The Pacific Dream...

A haven of

dazzling white sands

swaying coconut palms

and friendly smiles

Half the world's free water

A galaxy of coral atolls

in a sea of plenty

Food to fuel and heal

Resourcefulness

Flavours to inspire passion

Fresh, vibrant and heady

The palate of the Pacific

A spirit of freedom

Enchantment

This book is dedicated to the resourcefulness
and spirit of the Pacific peoples

An Annabel Langbein Book

First published in 2000 by The International Culinary Institute Press Ltd,
PO Box 99068 Newmarket, Auckland, New Zealand

ISBN 0-9582029-2-3

Design: Greg Dodds
Styling: Annabel Langbein
Copy editor: Helen Henry
Typesetting and production, ICIP: Natalie Keys
Printed in Hong Kong

SAVOUR THE PACIFIC

a discovery of taste

ANNABEL LANGBEIN

PHOTOGRAPHY KIERAN SCOTT

This book is my own cook's journey through the South Pacific. Inspired by extraordinarily resourceful people and a way of life far from the trappings of Western civilisation, I have attempted to unearth the lore and history behind the Pacific kitchen, and reveal some of the unique cultural and culinary rituals, many of which remain intact and are enjoyed to this day. I shared my travels with photographer Kieran Scott, whose evocative images have so wonderfully captured the free spirit of the region.

The recipes in this book do not represent the traditional cooking of the Pacific, which tends to be rather bland subsistence fare, but rather are my own interpretations as a cook – drawing on the wonderful palette of vibrant Pacific flavours, the influences of the diverse peoples who live there and their bountiful environment.

These simple, fresh recipes use ingredients easily found in supermarkets and specialty food stores. Before you start to cook, read the whole recipe through, gather everything you will need and then prepare the ingredients in the order they are listed. Feel comfortable about what you are setting out to achieve and the steps needed to get there.

Where practical, measures are given in cups and spoons.
A metric 250ml cup is used, 1 tsp = 5ml, 1 tbsp = 15ml. All conversions are approximate and have been rounded up or down for convenience. Follow one set of measurements; do not mix metric and imperial. While the recipes have been tested in a conventional oven, be aware that each oven will vary slightly and you may need to adjust cook times accordingly. If you use a fan-forced oven, the heat will be about 10-15% more powerful and food will cook more quickly.

Symbol ✪
This symbol is used throughout the book to indicate a recipe that can be found in another place. Check the index for the relevant page number.

break of day

In this brief moment of time, the air is cool and still. Inside the lagoon is a haven of glassy waters, while far on the outer reef the sea pounds its timeless rhythm. Through the dawn, the toll of church bells call early-morning service.

Vendors rattle their way to market laden with harvests. There are bananas – green and yellow – fresh papaya, huge shaggy tubers of taro and bunched taro leaves, cassava, chillies, snake beans and all things coconut.

Outboard engines roar into life as fishermen head out through the outer reef, breaking through spume and spindrift in search of the big fish. For those who have no worries, there is still a moment to dream – until it's time for breakfast.

MANGO
(mangifera indica)

Native to Southeast Asia, this
fragrant fruit is high in fibre,
rich in vitamins A and C and an
excellent source of potassium.
Fragrance is the best test of
ripeness and quality – no hint
of aroma usually means a
tasteless mango. Ripen at
room temperature – once ripe,
mangos can be kept in the
fridge for a few days.
The best way to get at the fruit
is to slice off the 'cheeks' on
either side of the stone.
With a small knife, score the
flesh in a criss-cross pattern
and then either scoop out with
a spoon or press the skin so
the cut side pops out – the
cubes can then be cut off the
skin. Green mango flesh
can be shredded into salads
and makes excellent chutneys;
fresh, ripe mangos are divine
eaten on their own.

fresh mango smoothie

• Prepare: 5 minutes • Serves 4

Canned or fresh mango can be used to make
this smooth, creamy 'meal in a drink'.

1 cup mango purée (flesh 1 ripe mango)
1½ cups apricot yoghurt
1½ cups fresh orange juice
1 tbsp lemon juice
a few ice cubes

BLEND all ingredients, except the ice, in a food
processor until smooth and creamy. Serve at
once over ice.

tutti frutti smoothie

• Prepare: 5 minutes
• Makes 4 small or 2 large smoothies

Passionfruit adds a delicious, tropical flavour to
this smoothie. See my wonderfully simple
recipe for Preserved Passionfruit Syrup✪, useful
when fresh passionfruit are out of season.

1 cup chopped mixed fresh fruit (eg. pineapple.
kiwifruit, melon, feijoas)
1 tbsp Preserved Passionfruit Syrup✪ or
passionfruit pulp
1 ripe banana. peeled
1 cup plain low-fat yoghurt
2 cups fresh orange juice
2 tbsp liquid honey or maple syrup. to taste
a few ice cubes

BLEND all ingredients, except the ice, in a food
processor until smooth. Serve at once over ice.

grilled tamarillos

- **Prepare: 2 minutes, plus standing**
- **Cook: 5-8 minutes • Serves 6**

Split, sprinkled with a little sugar and quickly grilled, these flavoursome fruits make a terrific breakfast or dessert. Serve with Pacific Muesli✿ and yoghurt.

6 ripe tamarillos

1/3 cup brown sugar

CUT tamarillos in half lengthwise. Place on a baking tray and sprinkle liberally with brown sugar. Leave to stand for at least 15 minutes.

HEAT grill. Place tamarillos on the second-to-top shelf, about 30cm (12in) from heat source.

GRILL for 5-8 minutes until surface starts to bubble and brown on the top and the fruit has softened.

mango passion sauce

- **Prepare: 2-3 minutes • Makes nearly 2 cups** (enough for 10-12 serves)

A wonderful light sauce packed with luscious tropical flavour – ideal for a fresh fruit salad, over icecream or served with a hot, fruity, steamed pudding.

1 x 425g (15oz) can mangos in natural juice

1 tsp minced fresh ginger

1/3 cup Preserved Passionfruit Syrup✿

PUREE mango with its juice until smooth. Stir in ginger and passionfruit. Chill until ready to serve.

Cook's note: Sauce will keep in the fridge for about 5 days.

WEEKEND BRUNCH

- fresh fruit plate
  with limes

- corn fritters with
  avocado chilli salsa and
  fried spiced tomatoes
  or
- fijian potato omelette
  with eggplant kasundi

- coconut passion cake

TAMARILLO
(cyphomandra betecea)

A beautiful, though surprisingly sour fruit, even when ripe. A ripe tamarillo has a shrivelled stem and will give slightly when squeezed. The skins slip off when the fruit is cooked or blanched. Serve raw – sliced, sprinkled with brown sugar and macerated – or cook to use in sweet or savoury sauces. The fruit's meaty texture and acidity make a good foil for rich meats such as pork and game. Tamarillos also make great chutney.

28

fijian potato omelette

- Prepare: 10 minutes • Cook: 12-15 minutes
- Serves 6-8

About half the population of Fiji is Indian, so spicy curries are very popular. Here, an aromatic potato and pea mixture is combined with eggs and then cooked into a fat omelette. Serve in wedges, warm or cold – try it with Eggplant Kasundi✿.

2 tbsp flavourless oil (eg. grapeseed)

1 onion, peeled and finely chopped

2 tsp each mustard seeds and cumin seeds

1 tsp fennel seeds, crushed

1 tsp curry powder

pinch cayenne

2 cloves garlic, peeled and crushed

1 tsp minced fresh ginger

4 medium-large peeled, diced and cooked potatoes

1 cup peas (can use thawed, frozen peas)

6 eggs

1 tsp salt

freshly ground black pepper

HEAT oil in a large, heavy frypan and gently fry onion, spices, garlic and ginger over low heat for about 10 minutes. Remove from heat and mix in potatoes and peas.

BEAT eggs in a large bowl. Add the spiced vegetables to the eggs and combine evenly. Season well.

LIGHTLY re-oil the pan. Pour mixture back into pan and cook over very low heat for 8-10 minutes, taking care omelette doesn't burn. As it cooks, heat grill. To finish off, place omelette under grill until it puffs and turns golden. Stand for 5 minutes before turning out. Allow to cool, then cut in wedges.

fijian potato omelette served with eggplant kasundi at top. grilled tamarillos with pacific muesli below

spiced poached fruits

- Prepare: 5 minutes • Cook: about 10-15 minutes
- Serves 6-8

This fragrant, spiced syrup adds a rich and exotic flavour to many fruits. I've used nectarines, but you can try it with a variety of fruits – such as peaches, pears, plums, feijoas, figs, guavas and tamarillos. Add the firmest and largest fruit to the syrup first.

2 cups sugar

2 cups water

20 very thin slices peeled, fresh ginger

juice and finely grated rind 2 lemons (no pith)

4 cinnamon sticks

1 vanilla pod, split in half

6-8 nectarines

MAKE syrup by placing sugar, water, ginger, lemon juice and rind, and cinnamon sticks in a large pot. Scrape seeds from vanilla pod and add to syrup along with pod. Bring to a boil, stirring now and then until sugar dissolves. Boil for 5 minutes.

STAND fruit in the syrup and cook at a very low simmer until fruit is just tender – about 10-15 minutes depending on size and ripeness of fruit.

PLACE fruit in a serving bowl and ladle over the syrup.

Cook's notes:
- Syrup can be made in advance and will keep in the fridge in a covered container for weeks.
- Poached fruits will keep for over a week in the fridge.

pacific muesli

- Prepare: 5 minutes • Cook: 45 minutes
- Makes 15-17 cups

This crunchy blend of toasted grains and nuts makes a great start to the day. It's delicious served with Grilled Tamarillos✿ – or any fresh fruit – and a good spoonful of Greek yoghurt.

3 cups mixed seeds and nuts (eg. whole almonds, pumpkin seeds, sunflower seeds, cashew nuts, linseed, sesame seeds)

8 cups rolled oats

2 cups bran

2 cups coarse thread coconut (see pg 146)

2 tsp cinnamon

1/2 cup liquid honey

1 cup flavourless oil (eg. grapeseed)

2 tsp vanilla essence

2 cups mixed, chopped, dried fruits – eg. papaya, pineapple, banana (optional)

HEAT oven to 170°C (325°F/gas 3).

COMBINE seeds, nuts, rolled oats, bran, coconut and cinnamon in a very large mixing bowl.

HEAT honey until very runny and mix in oil and vanilla. Stir into dry ingredients to evenly combine.

SPREAD mixture into 2 large roasting dishes and bake in oven for about 45 minutes, stirring occasionally, until crisp and pale golden. Cool and mix through dried fruits.

Cook's note: This recipe makes a big jarful of muesli which will keep for weeks in an airtight container.

FISHING THE LAGOON

We are in the village of Dalomo,
a tiny settlement of thatched huts
on the east coast of Yasawa Island,
in the west of the Fiji group.
In the soft light of dawn, a band of
about 12 men is fishing the lagoon
with nets and spears. Their harvests
today form a large pile of tiny
silver fish on the rocks.
Sam, one of the fishermen, waves
a broad black hand over
the vast wilderness of ocean that
stretches out in front of us.
"This is our supermarket,"
he laughs. "It's the biggest
supermarket in the whole world."
We trail back down the beach to
the village. Sam lays a piece of
corrugated iron over a thin flame,
arranging the tiny fish neatly over
the ridges. After a few minutes he
turns the fish over. "There," he says,
"they're done. Now we put them in
the sun to dry, and tomorrow
morning all we have to do is
mix them with coconut milk.
It's Sunday tomorrow and we
don't do any work."

Yasawas, May 99

spiced porridge with palm sugar and dried fruits

• Prepare: 5 minutes • Cook: 5-10 minutes
• Serves 2

Fresh spices, gratings of palm sugar and dried fruits give this comforting staple a well-deserved update.

2 cups rolled oats

2 cups water

3 cups milk

$1/2$ tsp salt

1 tsp cinnamon

$1/4$ tsp ground nutmeg

bowl whipped cream, crème fraîche or yoghurt

1 small cake palm sugar (see pg 143), grated, or $1/2$ cup brown sugar

small bowl dried fruits (eg. mango, papaya, banana and cranberry)

PLACE oats in a pot with water, milk, salt, cinnamon and nutmeg. Bring to the boil and simmer gently for 5-10 minutes, stirring often, until oats are cooked through and creamy. (If the porridge is too thick, add a little more milk or water to your liking.)

SERVE hot porridge in bowls with a spoonful of cream, crème fraîche or yoghurt, a few gratings of palm sugar or brown sugar and a sprinkle of dried fruits.

sweet-potato and salmon hash

• Prepare: 15 minutes • Cook: 16-20 minutes (per batch) • Serves 6

There's no need to wait around for leftovers to make these wonderful hash cakes. They're great for a special breakfast or brunch, topped with a soft poached egg.

2 large potatoes, peeled and chopped into large chunks

1 large sweet potato, peeled and chopped into large chunks

$1/2$ red pepper, deseeded, pith removed and chopped

200g (7oz) sliced smoked salmon or flaked smoked fish

1 small red chilli, deseeded, pith removed and minced

1 spring onion, finely chopped

2-3 tbsp chopped coriander (optional)

1 tsp salt

freshly ground black pepper

2 tbsp oil

BOIL potatoes and sweet potato in lightly salted water until tender. Drain and allow to cool.

MASH potatoes coarsely. Mix in red pepper, fish, chilli, spring onions and coriander. Season to taste.

DIVIDE mixture into 6 balls and flatten each slightly to form thick discs. (Hash can be prepared to this point and chilled ahead of time.)

HEAT oil in a large, heavy frypan. Fry hash cakes, 2-3 at a time, over medium heat for 8-10 minutes on each side until golden and crisp.

Variation: Use sliced, cooked corned beef in place of the smoked salmon.

coconut and banana flapjacks

- **Prepare: 10 minutes, plus standing**
- **Cook: 4-5 minutes (per batch)**
- **Makes 12 (serves 4-6)**

These thick, tender flapjacks, flavoured with coconut and banana, are great topped with grilled bacon, sliced bananas and maple syrup or Preserved Passionfruit Syrup✿.

2 eggs, separated

2 cups milk

$1/_2$ cup sugar

1 tsp vanilla essence

2 cups plain flour

3 tsp baking powder

$1/_2$ tsp salt

$1/_2$ cup coarse thread coconut (see pg 146), lightly toasted

1 ripe banana, peeled and mashed

flavourless oil (eg. grapeseed) for frying

BEAT egg yolks (reserve whites), milk, sugar and vanilla. Combine flour, baking powder and salt, add to egg mixture and beat until smooth. Mix in the coconut and banana. Leave to stand for at least 15 minutes or up to 3 hours in the fridge.

WHISK egg whites to soft peaks and gently fold into mixture.

HEAT a lightly oiled frypan. Spoon ladlefuls of batter into pan, 2-3 at a time, and cook over a medium heat for a couple of minutes. Flip flapjacks to cook other side once the bubbles that form on the top start to pop.

Variation: To make plain flapjacks, leave out the banana and coconut and add another 2 tbsp flour.

Cook's note: These flapjacks can be made in advance and reheated in the oven or microwave.

fresh fruit plate

- **Prepare: 10 minutes • Serves 6**

Choose a selection of fresh tropical fruits, such as papaya, melon and pineapple, for this simple platter. If you're using fruits that discolour quickly – say bananas and cherimoyas – prepare them immediately before serving.

$1/_2$ green melon

1 papaya

$1/_2$ fresh pineapple

2-3 limes or lemons

PEEL and deseed melon and papaya. Peel and core pineapple. (This can be done in advance and fruits chilled.)

SLICE fruit very thinly. Arrange on plates and accompany with a wedge of lime or lemon.

tropical yoghurt

- **Prepare: 5 minutes • Makes 3 cups**

This is a delicious accompaniment to a bowl of fresh fruit.

2 cups unsweetened yoghurt

2 tbsp liquid honey

$1/_2$ cup toasted thread coconut (see pg 146)

2 tbsp passionfruit pulp or Preserved Passionfruit Syrup✿

$1/_2$ cup finely chopped pineapple or crushed canned pineapple

FOLD ingredients together. Chill until serving.

Cook's notes:
- If using passionfruit pulp, you may need to add a little extra honey.
- Keeps for up to a week in the fridge

fresh lime at top,
fresh fruit plate below

LIME
(citrus latifolia)

This tropical member of the citrus family has a cool, wonderfully refreshing acidity. The rind and juice have superb flavours, but the white pith under the skin is bitter and should be removed. A zesting tool is ideal for removing strips of skin without pith. Store limes in a cool place, but don't refrigerate as they dry out.

Limes – vital freshness

Juicy limes feel heavy and 'give' when gently squeezed. Lime syrup makes a refreshing base for cool drinks: combine equal parts juice and sugar and the finely grated peel of half a lime. Stand for 12 hours, then boil with a little water, strain and cool. Pour over ice with a splash of bitters and top with soda or sparkling mineral water.

vanilla french toast with bananas, bacon and maple syrup

- Prepare: 5 minutes • Cook: 10-12 minutes
- Makes 8 (serves 4)

If you're serving this for a crowd, or just prefer to avoid last-minute cooking, prepare the toast ahead of time and reheat in a hot oven on a tray for 5-8 minutes to crisp up.

$^1/_2$ cup milk

1 tbsp sugar

3 eggs

1 tsp vanilla essence

finely grated rind of $^1/_2$ orange

8 finger-thick slices of 1 day old bread, eg, French bread, ciabatta, or white bread

1 tbsp butter

1 tbsp flavourless oil (eg, grapeseed)

2 firm bananas

4 rashers grilled bacon

maple syrup, to taste

BEAT milk with sugar to dissolve. Whisk in eggs, vanilla essence and orange rind.

DIP slices of bread into the liquid to coat both sides.

HEAT butter and oil in a large heavy frypan. Cook bread slices in batches, over a medium heat for 2-3 minutes each side, turning to cook other side as they brown. Keep warm and cook remaining bread slices (add more oil and butter if necessary).

ACCOMPANY each serving with several slices of firm banana (peeled and angle-sliced at the last minute), cooked bacon and maple syrup.

Variation: Sprinkle cooked French toast with cinnamon sugar and serve with fresh fruits instead of bacon and maple syrup.

BANANA

(musa paradisiaca)

Bananas are a prolific Pacific food source. Green bananas are widely consumed as a starch – roasted, steamed, fried or mixed into curries. Ripe bananas are a rich source of potassium and extremely digestible – ideal for athletes, the young and elderly. For peak flavour, ripen off the plant. Most bananas sold in the West are dessert bananas, which go mushy when cooked. The small 'ladyfinger' fruits keep their shape when cooked; otherwise, for green cooking bananas, check out Asian, Pacific or Latin American markets. The crimson flowers make attractive serving baskets; they can also be served as a vegetable, thinly sliced and cooked. Banana leaves, while inedible, make good wrappers for grilled or baked foods, and give a fragrant taste to the food cooked inside.

corn fritters

- Prepare: 10 minutes, plus standing
- Cook: 2-3 minutes (per batch)
- Makes 10-12 (serves 5-6)

Fresh corn cut from the cob, frozen (thawed) or canned corn can be used for these flavoursome fritters. They make a filling breakfast or lunch served with rocket leaves, Avocado Chilli Salsa✿ and Fried Spiced Tomatoes✿.

- 1½ cups plain flour
- 3 tsp baking powder
- 3 eggs
- 1 tsp salt
- freshly ground black pepper
- ¾ cup chilled soda water or cold water
- 2½ -3 cups corn kernels
- 3 tbsp chopped fresh mint or coriander
- 1 tsp minced red chilli (optional)
- flavourless oil (eg. grapeseed) for frying

COMBINE flour, baking powder, eggs, salt and pepper and soda water or water to a smooth batter. Mix in corn kernels, mint or coriander and chilli. Stand for 5-10 minutes before cooking (up to 2 hours in the fridge).

HEAT a spoonful of oil in a heavy frypan. Cook large spoonfuls of the mixture, 2-3 at a time, over medium heat, turning to cook the other side as bubbles form in the mixture. Lightly re-oil pan between batches. Transfer cooked fritters to a rack.

Cook's note: These fritters can be made ahead of time and reheated in a hot oven for 5 minutes. They can also be cooked in tiny spoonfuls and served as finger food.

vanilla french toast with bananas, bacon and maple syrup at top; corn fritters with avocado chilli salsa and fried spiced tomatoes below

Thousands of years ago, before Nordic canoes made their first forays to the shores of Britain, courageous voyagers in sophisticated ocean-going canoes were navigating the Pacific. Filtering East from Asia, they reached Tonga and Samoa by 1000 BC, establishing, over the following centuries, a triangle of culture on remote islands and atolls between Hawaii, New Zealand and Easter Island. These people came to be known as the

Polynesians – 'people of many islands'. In the West, in a band that runs from New Guinea across to the Solomons through to Fiji, lives a more ancient people – the broad-faced, dark-skinned Melanesians, whose hunter-gatherer roots go back to the region of Java. The area to the north-west, defined in linguistic and cultural terms as Micronesia, has predominantly Asian influences. Over the centuries these cultures have evolved to create a many-faceted Pacific culture.

a daily rhythm

morning refreshments

There is work to be done: gardens to tend, crops to harvest and store, pigs to hunt, wild nuts and fruits to gather, mats to weave and children to care for. And always – day after day, year after year – there are fish to catch.

Life's daily rhythm flows in simple ordered tasks under the watchful gaze of chief and church.

Tiny children man dug-out canoes and make out across the divide of open ocean to the missionary school, braving sea and sharks for a dose of Christian doctrine.

As the heat rises and the morning's toils raise a bead of sweat to the brow, it is time to crack open a fresh green coconut, pause and savour its cool refreshing draft.

tropical fruit slice

• Prepare: 20 minutes • Makes about 48 pieces

A variety of dried fruits can be used for this no-cook slice, but make sure at least half the fruit has a good acidic flavour – such as apricots – or else the slice will be too sweet.

100g (4oz) butter

$^2/_3$ cup ($^1/_2$ x 397g/14oz can) sweetened condensed milk

1 x 250g (9oz) packet plain sweet biscuits, crushed to crumbs (about 2$^1/_2$ cups)

2 cups roughly chopped dried fruits (eg, apricots, papaya, pineapple)

1 cup desiccated coconut (see pg 146)

2 tbsp lemon juice

Lemon Icing: 50g (2oz) butter, melted; 3 tbsp boiling water; 1 tbsp lemon juice; 3$^1/_2$ cups icing sugar

MELT butter and condensed milk, stirring over heat until it boils. Remove from heat.

ADD crushed biscuits, dried fruit (reserving $^1/_4$ cup for decoration), coconut and lemon juice. Mix well and press into a 30cm x 24cm (12in x 9in) baking tin. Refrigerate until set.

MAKE icing by mixing all ingredients to a smooth paste. Ice slice and sprinkle with reserved dried fruits. Chill until set (about an hour) then cut into bars.

Cook's note: This tropical fruit slice will keep for several weeks in an airtight container.

PAPAYA
(carica papaya)

In the steamy heat of the tropics, the statuesque papaya grows like a weed, producing fruit from seed in less than 10 months and cropping continuously for about 18. Known also as pawpaw, fruta bomba and tree melon, this nutritious fruit (it is an excellent source of vitamins A and C and is rich in potassium) can be pear-shaped or round. Green papaya can be served raw in a salad or cooked as a vegetable. Ripe fruit needs nothing more than a squeeze of fresh lime juice. Papaya seeds are a potent laxative. The fruit also contains a substance which interferes with human progesterone, so women wishing to conceive or in the early stages of pregnancy should avoid it. Green papaya has a thick white sap under the skin which is used locally to treat insect bites and inflammations.

sugar lime cookies

- Prepare: 10 minutes • Cook: 25-30 minutes
- Makes about 36 crisp biscuits

Citrus rinds contain flavoursome oils, while the underlying white pith is bitter. Use a zesting tool to remove rinds without pith, or cut thin strips with a vegetable peeler and remove any pith.

> 125g (4$\frac{1}{2}$oz) butter, softened, plus extra for greasing trays
>
> finely grated rind 3 limes (no pith)
>
> 1$\frac{1}{2}$ cups caster sugar
>
> 1 egg
>
> 1$\frac{3}{4}$ cups plain flour
>
> $\frac{1}{2}$ tsp baking soda
>
> $\frac{1}{2}$ tsp vanilla essence
>
> 2-3 drops pure lime or lemon oil (optional)

HEAT oven to 150°C (300°F/gas 2) and lightly grease baking trays with butter.

PLACE rind on a chopping board with 3 tbsp of the caster sugar and chop finely to release oils from the rinds into sugar. Place half this mixture to one side as a topping for biscuits.

COMBINE other half of lime-flavoured sugar with remaining sugar and butter and beat for a couple of minutes. In a mixer or by hand, beat in egg, then add flour, baking soda, vanilla essence and lime or lemon oil, mixing until a smooth dough is formed. (Use enough flour so that the dough comes away from the sides of the bowl. It will be slightly sticky and quite soft but manageable.)

FORM small balls of dough and flatten onto baking trays. Sprinkle tops with the reserved sugar-and-rind mixture and bake in the oven for about 25-30 minutes until pale golden and crisp. Allow to cool on tray, then remove and store in an airtight container.

SPICED TEAS

Fragrant spiced tea is a feature of the Fijian table. It can be made with a variety of spices – the Indians in Fiji always include black pepper. I like to make it by the potful: place a tablespoon of black tea leaves in a warmed pot, add a stick of cinnamon, 8 peppercorns, 4 crushed cardamom pods, a tablespoon of grated fresh ginger, a grating of fresh whole nutmeg and a squeeze of fresh lime juice. Pour over boiling water, leave to brew for a few minutes and serve with a spoonful of honey.
For spiced coconut tea, a quarter-cup of toasted coconut can be used in place of the tea leaves.

freda's nutty crisps

- Prepare: 10 minutes • Cook: 20 minutes
- Makes about 28 biscuits

These wafer-thin, super-crisp biscuits are great for mid-morning snacking.

125g (4^1/$_2$oz) butter, softened, plus extra for greasing trays

^{1}/$_2$ cup sugar

2 tsp golden syrup

^{1}/$_4$ tsp baking soda, dissolved in 1 tsp hot water

^{1}/$_2$ tsp baking powder

2 tsp dry ginger

1 cup plain flour

^{1}/$_2$ cup very finely chopped walnut pieces or macadamias

HEAT oven to 150°C (300°F/gas 2) and lightly grease baking trays with butter.

BEAT remaining butter with sugar until creamy. Beat in golden syrup, then mix in the baking soda, the dry ingredients and nuts, mixing until dough comes away from the sides of the bowl.

FORM small balls of dough and flatten hard onto prepared trays. Bake in oven for 20 minutes until crisp, flattening again with a fork or the palm of your hand after 5 minutes of cooking time to make very thin biscuits. Transfer cooked biscuits to a rack to cool, then store in an airtight container.

Cook's note: Flour quality varies depending on humidity, age and type. These factors can affect the flour's take-up of water. It's one of those ingredients where you can follow the recipe exactly and end up with differing results. Use flour types specified in individual recipes and familiarise yourself with the consistency of different mixtures.

spiced teas at top; the perfect sun shade, Yasawa Islands, below

spiced fruit loaf

• Prepare: 10 minutes • Cook: 1 hour, 30 minutes
• Makes 1 large loaf

This wonderfully moist loaf slices like a dream and will keep fresh for over a week if stored in an airtight container. Try also as a pudding served hot with custard.

50g (2oz) butter, softened, plus extra for greasing tin

$1/4$ cup glacé ginger, roughly chopped

$1 1/2$ cups (tightly packed) chopped, pitted dates

$1 1/4$ cups water

1 tbsp golden syrup

1 cup sugar

1 tsp mixed spice

$1/2$ tsp grated nutmeg

$1 1/2$ tsp ground ginger

1 cup chopped dried papaya or apricots

$1/2$ cup chopped brazil nuts or walnuts (optional)

1 tsp vanilla essence

pinch salt

2 cups plain flour

1 tsp baking soda

1 tsp baking powder

Topping: 12 whole brazil nuts or almonds, 2-3 tbsp chopped dried papaya or other dried fruits

HEAT oven to 150°C (300°F/gas 2) and grease a 23cm x 14cm (9in x 6in) loaf tin with butter.

PLACE glacé ginger and dates in a pot with the water, golden syrup, sugar and remaining butter. Boil 5 minutes, mash lightly to break up dates, then remove from heat and leave to cool.

MIX in remaining ingredients (except those for topping). Spoon mixture into tin, sprinkle over topping ingredients and bake 1 hour 30 minutes, or until a skewer inserted in centre comes out clean and the top is springy to the touch. Leave to cool, then turn out.

ginger crunch

• Prepare: 15 minutes • Cook: 18-20 minutes
• Makes 24 squares

With a crisp shortcrust base and fudgy ginger topping, this easy slice is a classic favourite. Stored in an airtight container, it will keep fresh for about 2 weeks.

125g ($4 1/2$oz) butter, plus extra for greasing tin

$1/2$ cup sugar

$1 1/3$ cups plain flour

2 tsp ground ginger

1 tsp baking powder

Topping: 100g (4oz) butter, $1 1/2$ cups icing sugar, 3 tbsp golden syrup, 4 tsp ground ginger

HEAT oven to 180°C (350°F/gas 4) and grease a 23cm x 30cm (9in x 12in) shallow sponge roll or baking tin with butter.

BEAT remaining butter and sugar until creamy. Sift together flour, ginger and baking powder, add to butter and sugar and mix until evenly combined and ingredients come together in a softish ball.

POUR mixture into the prepared tin and press firmly to even out. Bake for 18-20 minutes until pale golden.

PLACE topping ingredients in a pot or microwave bowl. Heat until melted, stir to combine evenly and spread over cooked base while still hot. Cut into squares while still warm.

spiced fruit loaf at top,
fresh nutmeg kernels below

NUTMEG

(myristca fragrans)

The seed of the nutmeg tree lies inside a lacy covering – or aril – of scarlet mace. Encased in a shell, the seed is very hard and requires a fine grater to extract the aromatic spice. The oil is used as a sedative and the spice has a long history of use as a digestive.

Nutmeg - to calm and warm

Nutmeg has a warm spicy flavour that goes well with sweet baking and fruits, as well as spinach, onions, mushrooms and chicken. Mace flavour hints more of cinnamon and peppercorns. While its taste is slightly different from nutmeg, it goes well with the same ingredients. It's also one of the few spices that keeps its flavour for a long period when ground.

A TASTE FOR
HUMAN FLESH

Anthropophagy was part of daily life for the many different peoples of the Pacific, lasting, in some remote areas, well into the past century. On the hill above Sigatoka township in Fiji, a huge cooking pot stands testimony to the local appetite for 'long pig'.

The last recorded act of cannibalism was in 1969 among the Big Nambas, on the island of Malekula in Vanuatu, supposedly the last tribe to convert to Christianity.

The Reverend Thomas Williams' account of Fijian life in 1852 includes 10 pages of text on the many local practices of cannibalism. Williams writes: "A Chief would kill a man or men on laying down the keel for a new canoe, and try to add one for each fresh plank. These were always eaten as 'food for the carpenters'."

pacific pot sticker and pizza dough

• **Prepare**: 10 minutes, plus rising • Makes enough for 24 individual dumplings or pizzas

This multi-purpose dough, with its slightly sweet flavour, is commonly used in Chinese breads and dumplings. It's a cinch to make and is perfect for Pacific Pot Stickers✪ and Mini Pacific Pizzas✪.

2 tbsp sugar

1 cup warm (not hot) water

1$\frac{1}{2}$ tbsp dried yeast

$\frac{1}{2}$ cup milk

2 tbsp flavourless oil (eg. grapeseed)

about 3$\frac{1}{2}$ cups high-grade flour

1 tsp salt

PLACE sugar, water and yeast in a large mixing bowl. Leave for about 5 minutes until yeast softens and starts to froth. Mix in milk and oil, then 3 cups of the flour and salt, mixing with a knife until all flour is absorbed.

TURN OUT dough onto a lightly floured board and knead lightly until smooth, adding the remaining flour as needed to form a soft, slightly sticky dough.

COVER and leave to rise in a warm place for about 30 minutes or until doubled in size. Dough is now ready to use.

Cook's note: Prepared dough will keep in a clean plastic bag in the fridge for a couple of days or can be frozen.

pacific pot stickers (pg 50)

pacific pot stickers

- Prepare: 15 minutes, plus standing
- Cook: 10 minutes to steam, plus 2-3 minutes to fry • Makes 30

These tasty dumplings can be steamed ahead of time and quickly fried off at serving time.

> 1 tbsp oil
>
> 400g (14oz) pork mince or chicken mince
>
> 1 tsp minced fresh ginger
>
> 2 spring onions, finely chopped
>
> 3 tbsp hoisin or oyster sauce
> (see *Cook's note*, right, and pg 130)
>
> 2 tbsp Thai sweet chilli sauce
>
> 2 tbsp chopped fresh coriander
>
> salt and freshly ground black pepper
>
> 1 recipe Pacific Pot Sticker and Pizza Dough✿
>
> 1 tsp each sesame oil and flavourless oil
> (eg. grapeseed) to fry

HEAT 1 tbsp oil and fry mince with ginger to brown. Remove from heat and mix in onions, sauces and coriander. Season to taste. Cool.

ASSEMBLE dumplings by rolling dough into a long sausage shape. Divide into 30 equal pieces. Roll each piece of dough into a round of about 10cm (4in) diameter. Place a tablespoon of filling in the middle of each round. Pull up dough in small pleats to enclose filling, pinching edges firmly at the top to seal securely.

CUT dumpling-sized rounds of baking paper. Sit each dumpling on a paper round in a large steamer basket, allowing 2-3cm (1in) space between each. Leave to rise for 15 minutes, then cook in a hot covered steamer for 10 minutes.

REMOVE dumplings from steamer. When ready to serve, quickly fry in a frypan heated with combined oils until golden on each side.

Cook's note: The filling mixture can be made a day ahead of time and chilled in the fridge. The dumplings can be shaped and frozen raw; in which case steam for 15 minutes from frozen.

mini pacific pizzas

- Prepare: 10 minutes • Cook: 15 minutes
- Makes for 24-30 mini pizzas

Thai sweet chilli, hoisin or oyster sauce makes a great flavour-base for a range of Pacific-style pizzas, and a delicious change from tomato. Good-quality commercial pizza bases are also yummy with this combination of toppings.

> 1 recipe Pacific Pot Sticker and Pizza Dough✿
>
> $1/2$ cup hoisin or oyster (see pg 130) sauce
>
> 2 tbsp Thai sweet chilli sauce
>
> 2 cups shredded cooked duck (see pg 132)
> or chicken
>
> 2 spring onions, finely sliced on an angle
>
> salt and freshly ground black pepper

HEAT oven to 220°C (425°F/gas 7). Grease or line 2-3 baking trays.

DIVIDE dough into 24-30 pieces. Flatten into thin rounds and spread out on prepared trays.

COMBINE hoisin or oyster sauce and chilli sauce. Place half of this in a bowl, add the duck or chicken and spring onions and mix through to combine.

SPREAD remaining sauce over pizza bases. Season with salt and pepper. Bake for 10 minutes, then top with the shredded duck or chicken and cook a further 5 minutes.

Cook's note: Hoisin sauce is a thick, sweet, strongly flavoured brownish-red sauce made from soy beans, vinegar, sugar and spices, including star anise. Once opened, store in the fridge.

vegetable samosas served with tropical fruit chutney at top, mini pacific pizzas below

vegetable samosas

- Prepare: 20 minutes • Cook: 15-20 minutes
- Makes 20 small samosas

The spicy vegetable filling used for these tasty snacks is sensational. Use it also as a filling for stuffed potatoes. Serve with Tamarind Dipping Sauce❂ or Tropical Fruit Chutney❂.

Spice Mix: 1 tbsp oil; 1 onion, peeled and finely chopped; 2 tsp mustard seeds; 2 tsp ground cumin; 1 tsp curry powder; $^1/_4$ tsp cayenne; 2 cloves garlic, peeled and crushed

1 cooked potato, peeled and chopped

$^1/_2$ carrot, peeled and grated

$^1/_4$ cup peas (can use thawed, frozen peas)

$^1/_2$ cup chopped coriander

salt and freshly ground black pepper

40 squares (7cm x 7cm/3in x 3in) of wonton pastry (see pg 102)

beaten egg and a few sesame seeds to glaze

FRY the Spice Mix ingredients over low heat for 10 minutes. Combine with potato, carrot, peas and coriander. Season to taste.

HEAT oven to 190°C (375°F/gas 5). Grease or line a baking tray.

JOIN 2 square sheets of wonton dough together to form a rectangle (seal join with water). With the long side facing you, place a teaspoon of the vegetable mixture in the centre of the left-hand side. Now take the bottom left-hand corner and bring it over the filling to form a triangle (which will meet where the two wonton sheets join). Now fold that triangle over the right-hand wonton sheet. Finally, bring the bottom right-hand corner of the right wonton sheet over the filled triangle. Use a little water to seal the join. Continue with remaining wonton sheets and filling.

PLACE parcels on prepared tray. Brush tops with beaten egg and sprinkle with sesame seeds. Bake for about 15-20 minutes until crisp and golden. Serve hot or at room temperature.

rhubarb and ginger muffins

- Prepare: 5 minutes • Cook: 15 minutes
- Makes 12

These light, tender muffins freeze well.

100g (4oz) butter, melted, plus extra for greasing tins

1 cup sugar

2 eggs

$\frac{1}{2}$ tsp baking soda

$\frac{1}{2}$ cup milk, warmed

1 tsp vanilla essence

2 cups finely chopped raw rhubarb

2 tbsp finely chopped glacé ginger

2 cups self-raising flour

2 tsp ground ginger

Topping (optional): $\frac{1}{4}$ cup honey; 1 tbsp butter;
$\frac{1}{2}$ cup chopped, lightly toasted macadamias

HEAT oven to 200°C (400°F/gas 6) and lightly butter 12 muffin tins.

BEAT together butter, sugar and eggs. Dissolve baking soda in the warm milk and add to the butter and sugar mixture, along with the vanilla essence, rhubarb and glacé ginger. Fold in flour and ground ginger, mixing until just combined (do not over-mix).

DIVIDE mixture between muffin tins and bake in oven for 15 minutes or until risen and golden.

MAKE topping by placing honey, butter and nuts in a pot and boiling for 1 minute (or 2 minutes on HIGH in the microwave). Spoon over cooked muffins. Stand for 5-10 minutes before removing from tins.

Variation: Use $1\frac{1}{2}$ cups mashed banana or chopped feijoa in place of rhubarb, leave out ginger and add 1 tsp cinnamon and $\frac{1}{4}$ cup chopped walnuts.

loading a dugout with the day's harvests, Malekula Island, at top; rhubarb and ginger muffins below

banana cake

• Prepare: 15 minutes • Cook: 1 hour
• Makes 1 large cake (about 10-12 servings)

This moist, light cake is a great way to use up very ripe bananas. It's great for morning tea or an easy dessert. Serve with whipped cream and dried bananas, or try it with Lemon Icing✿.

250g (9oz) butter, softened

1¹/₂ cups sugar

4 eggs

2 tsp vanilla essence

4 ripe bananas, peeled and mashed (about 2 cups)

2 tsp baking soda

¹/₂ cup hot milk

2 tsp baking powder

3 cups plain flour, sifted

HEAT oven to 170°C (325°F/gas 3). Line a 25cm (10in) cake tin with baking paper.

BEAT butter and sugar until creamy. Beat in eggs, vanilla, then bananas. Dissolve baking soda in hot milk and add to mixture. Combine baking powder with flour and fold into cake mix.

SPOON cake batter into prepared tin and smooth top. Bake for 1 hour or until a skewer inserted in the centre comes out clean and the top is springy to the touch. Cool in tin before turning out.

Cook's notes:
• This cake freezes well (without the icing).
• Very ripe bananas can be frozen in their skins, thawed and peeled for use in cakes, muffins and drinks.

banana cake at top, young bananas emerging from edible banana flower below

PINEAPPLE

(ananas comosus)

The divine lusciousness of a ripe pineapple is an elusive pleasure. All too often, we are faced with fruit with insipid taste and little sweetness – testimony to the fact that pineapples don't continue to ripen once they have been picked.

Choose a heavy, firm fruit that smells sweetly aromatic (rather than in a state of ferment). Pull a leaf from the crown – if it comes out easily the fruit is ripe.

Pineapples contain the enzyme bromelin, similar to that found in papaya and kiwifruit, which breaks down protein. For this reason, pineapple is often used as a tenderiser for meat. Unless the fruit or juice is cooked, this enzyme prevents jellies made with gelatine from setting. This same enzyme is thought to be very helpful for digestion – in Hawaii a plateful of fresh pineapple is prescribed as a cure for digestive problems.

coconut passion cake

- Prepare: 10 minutes • Cook: 1 hour
- Makes 1 large cake (about 16 servings)

This delicious cake can be made with a variety of fruits (see *Variation*, below) and keeps fresh for over a week. It looks very special decorated with Candied Hibiscus Flowers✿.

$1^3/_4$ cups sugar

150g (5oz) butter

4 eggs

2 cups desiccated coconut (see pg 146)

2 cups self-raising flour

1 tsp baking powder

$1/_2$ cup coconut cream or milk

$1/_4$ cup Preserved Passionfruit Syrup✿

Passionfruit Butter Icing: 50g (2oz) butter, softened; 3 tbsp passionfruit pulp; 3 cups icing sugar; $1/_2$ tbsp hot water

HEAT oven (don't use fan setting) to 180°C (350°F/gas 4). Line a 25cm (10in) cake tin with baking paper to cover base and sides.

BEAT sugar and butter until creamy. Beat in eggs one at a time. Combine coconut, flour and baking powder and fold into mixture, alternating with the combined coconut cream or milk and Preserved Passionfruit Syrup.

POUR mixture into prepared cake tin and smooth top. Bake for 1 hour or until skewer inserted into the centre comes out clean. Cool and remove from tin.

PREPARE icing while cake cooks: beat together butter, passionfruit pulp, icing sugar and hot water until creamy and evenly mixed. Spread over top of cooled cake. Store in a cool place.

Variation: Add 1 cup peeled, chopped feijoas – or other acid fruit, such as plums, apricots or berries – into batter when adding Preserved Passionfruit Syrup.

coconut passion cake decorated
with candied hibiscus flowers

Everything needed for a new way of life was carefully packed for the long sea journeys of the early Polynesians. For short trips, their sturdy vessels could carry up to 100 passengers. Planned migrations to new territory involved a strong sense of courage and determination. Up to 40 people per boat, with little more than woven mats for shelter and warmth, endured the searing heat of the tropics by day and freezing desert-like nights.

Pounders and digging sticks for taro, sennit fishnets, bone and pearl fish hooks, wooden spears, slingshots for birds, and fine woven mats – all the essentials to start afresh in new lands were stored inside the canoes. Taro, breadfruit, yams, bananas, pandanus leaves, gourds, coconuts, sugar cane, dogs, chickens, rats and pigs were all introduced by these early voyagers.

lunch in the shade
of a coconut tree

Dexterous fingers work with fluid speed, moulding a banana leaf into a bowl for washing hands, coconut fronds into food containers, narrow tubes of bamboo into drinking vials.

While the women prepare food under thatched cover in the cooking hut, the men sit outside, playing the tamtam and singing the old songs.

As the air starts to cool in late afternoon, with chores complete, the family gathers to share the day's meal. Sitting on soft pandanus mats, they take turns to break off pieces of food, dipping them into the rich coconut milk. Elders and children eat first; the women eat last, often alone.

No matter the occasion, there is always food to share.

spicy pumpkin soup

- **Prepare:** 10 minutes • **Cook:** 30 minutes
- **Serves 4**

In subsistence island lifestyles, pumpkin is often served cooked with coconut milk. The addition of aromatics such as chillies, lemongrass, fish sauce and fresh coriander transform this simple soup into a special meal. Accompany with poppadoms.

2 tbsp olive oil

1 onion, peeled and finely chopped

1 tbsp brown sugar

2 cloves garlic, peeled and crushed

1.2kg (2$\frac{1}{2}$lb) pumpkin (eg. buttercup), deseeded, peeled and chopped

2 cups water

1 x 400g (14oz) can coconut milk

1-2 fresh or dried red chillies, deseeded, pith removed and finely chopped

1 tbsp minced lemongrass or $\frac{1}{2}$ tsp finely grated lemon rind (no pith)

1 tbsp fish sauce

salt and freshly ground black pepper

$\frac{1}{4}$ cup fresh coriander or parsley, chopped

HEAT oil in a large pot and gently cook onion, sugar and garlic for 8-10 minutes until softened.

ADD all other ingredients, except coriander or parsley, and simmer until pumpkin is tender (about 20 minutes).

MASH ingredients, adjust seasoning to taste and mix through coriander or parsley.

Variation: Prawns or diced fish can be added for a special occasion. Add to soup in the last 5 minutes of cooking.

SUMMER LUNCH

- coconut and coriander fish fritters

- satay chicken salad
  or
- vietnamese roast chicken noodle salad

- macadamia feuilleté with caramelised banana topping

hot and sour noodle soup

- Prepare: 10 minutes • Cook: 10 minutes
- Serves 4

Make your own stock in bulk and freeze, or buy fresh chilled stock from the supermarket. Don't use stock cubes.

5 cups tasty chicken stock

1 stalk lemongrass (or 1 tbsp dried)

finely grated rind 1 lime or lemon (no pith), plus 3 tbsp juice

4 thin slices galangal or fresh ginger

2-3 tsp Thai green curry paste, to taste

2 boneless, skinless chicken breasts cut in thin slices across the grain

2 handfuls fresh enoki mushrooms or 1 x 425g (15oz) can, drained

2 tbsp fish sauce

1 tbsp Tamarind Dipping Sauce✪ or ready-made tamarind sauce

250g (9oz) fresh rice noodles, or soaked dry rice noodles (optional)

$1/4$ cup chopped coriander

freshly ground black pepper

PLACE stock in a pot. Crush lemongrass at bulbous end with the back of a heavy knife to break up. Add to stock, along with the lime or lemon rind, galangal or ginger and curry paste. Bring to a simmer.

ADD chicken and mushrooms and cook over gentle heat for 5 minutes. Mix in fish sauce, lime or lemon juice, Tamarind Dipping Sauce or tamarind sauce and noodles. Simmer 2 minutes or until noodles are tender. Mix in coriander and black pepper. Serve straightaway.

Cook's note: Galangal is a member of the ginger family, bearing a rhizome with a flavour reminiscent of camphor. Available bottled in brine or dried in slices from Asian food stores. Use 2-3 slices in soups and sauces.

FISH SAUCE

The soy sauce of Southeast Asia, fish sauce is a pungent, salty brown liquid useful for flavouring everything savoury from stir-fries to salads and curries. It is made from fermented anchovies and other small fish. Don't be put off by its foul smell, this disappears completely when added to other ingredients and the zing of flavour it provides is fabulous. In general, the better the quality, the darker the colour of the sauce. Keeps indefinitely.

coconut chicken soup

- Prepare: 5 minutes • Cook: 20 minutes
- Serves 4

This is one of the simplest meal-in-a-soup dishes I know. It takes just 20 minutes from start to table.

4 cups chicken stock

1 x 400g (14oz) can coconut cream

1 small red chilli, deseeded, pith removed and finely minced

2 tbsp fresh lime or lemon juice

1 tbsp fish sauce

4 double kaffir lime leaves or 1 tsp minced lemongrass

$1/4$ cup long-grain or jasmine rice

2 boneless, skinless chicken breasts, sliced very thinly across the grain

2 tbsp chopped coriander

salt and freshly ground black pepper

HEAT together stock, coconut cream, chilli, lime or lemon juice and fish sauce in a pot. Add kaffir lime leaves or lemongrass with the rice and simmer for 12 minutes, stirring occasionally.

ADD chicken and simmer gently for 5 minutes until cooked through. Mix in coriander and season to taste with salt and pepper.

Cook's notes:
- Chicken needs to be thoroughly cooked, but will be done very quickly if thinly sliced. As with meat, slice across the grain for maximum tenderness.
- Jasmine rice is known for its fragrance – it is slightly sticky when cooked and remains delicious when reheated.

COCONUT KNOW-HOW

Two liquids come from a coconut: fresh coconut water or juice from the green coconut – so pure it can be used as a saline solution for an emergency drip – and coconut milk which is extracted from the flesh of mature coconuts.

The first 'press' of the flesh is usually sold in cans under the name of coconut cream. Quality varies greatly from brand to brand, with a very thick pouring consistency denoting premium quality. Avoid the small cans of solid coconut cream sold under Asian brand names as they are often rancid. Coconut milk can be made from fresh or dried coconut, although the flavour of fresh is far superior. To make a thick coconut milk, purée the grated flesh of a mature coconut – or 2 cups dried, desiccated coconut – with 1 cup hot water. Strain, squeezing all the liquid from the flesh. Chill and use within two days, or freeze.

satay chicken salad

• Prepare: 10 minutes • Serves 4

The aromatic dressing that coats this moist, crunchy salad is also delicious with fish and pork.

4 large handfuls watercress or mixed salad greens

1 green pepper, deseeded, pith removed and finely sliced

3 stalks celery, thinly sliced

2 poached chicken breasts, skin removed and sliced

2 spring onions, finely sliced

1 bunch long beans or green beans, boiled 2-3 minutes

$^1/_2$ cup roasted peanuts

$^1/_2$ cup chopped coriander

Satay Dressing: 1 tsp minced fresh ginger; 1 tsp crushed garlic; $^1/_2$ cup roasted peanuts; 1 cup coconut cream; juice and finely grated rind 1 lemon (no pith); 1 tsp minced red chilli; 2 double kaffir lime leaves, finely shredded (optional); salt and freshly ground black pepper

PLACE all ingredients, except those used in the dressing, in a large mixing bowl.

PUREE dressing ingredients until smooth and creamy and toss through salad. Serve at once.

Cook's notes: To poach chicken with a Pacific flavour, place chicken breasts in a single layer in a large pot. Cover with cold water, add 4-5 thin slices fresh ginger, 1 small red chilli, few peppercorns and a spring onion. Bring slowly to a simmer. Simmer for 5 minutes, then leave to cool in the cooking liquid.

satay chicken salad at top, tamtams below

vietnamese roast-chicken noodle salad

- Prepare: 10 minutes • Cook: 25-30 minutes
- Serves 4

This light, fresh salad, with its zing of mint leaves, makes great lunch fare. It travels well; pack it into a container for picnics or potlucks. If preferred, the chicken can be poached (see *Cook's notes*, opposite).

2-3 boneless chicken breasts (skin on)

salt and freshly ground black pepper

200g (7oz) dried rice sticks soaked in hot water for 10 minutes, or 400g (14oz) fresh rice noodles

about 16 snowpeas

1 red pepper, deseeded, pith removed and cut into thin strips

2 spring onions, finely sliced

100g (4oz) mung bean sprouts

$1/2$ cup (tightly packed) chopped mint

$1/4$ cup toasted sesame seeds

Vietnamese Dressing: $1/2$ cup Thai sweet chilli sauce; $1/4$ cup rice vinegar; 2 tbsp fish sauce; finely grated rind 1 lime or lemon (no pith), plus 2 tbsp juice; 2 double kaffir lime leaves, finely shredded (optional)

HEAT oven to 200°C (400°F/gas 6). Place chicken in a shallow roasting pan. Season and bake 25-30 minutes until cooked. Cool, remove and discard skin and shred flesh into bite-sized pieces.

BOIL soaked rice sticks or fresh noodles for 2 minutes until tender. Rinse under cold water and drain. Cover snowpeas with boiling water, leave 30 seconds and then rinse under cold water. Drain and slice thinly.

PLACE chicken, noodles and snowpeas in a large bowl with remaining salad ingredients. Combine dressing ingredients; toss through salad. Check seasoning and adjust to taste.

making lap lap (pg 97) at top, vietnamese roast-chicken noodle salad below

papaya, avocado and prawn salad with curry mayo

• Prepare: 10 minutes • Serves 6

Rarotongans make a divine salad using just papaya and curry mayonnaise. I've added prawns, avocado and mint for a stunningly simple light meal or first course.

> Curry Mayo: $\frac{1}{4}$ cup finely chopped mint leaves; $\frac{1}{2}$-1 tsp good-quality curry powder; $\frac{1}{2}$-1 red chilli, deseeded, pith removed and minced; 3 tbsp lime or lemon juice; 1 tbsp Thai sweet chilli sauce; $\frac{1}{2}$ cup homemade or good-quality commercial mayonnaise
>
> 500g (1lb) prawns, cooked and shelled
>
> 2 just-ripe avocados, peeled and flesh chopped
>
> 1 papaya or green melon, peeled, deseeded and flesh chopped
>
> salt and freshly ground black pepper
>
> rocket or soft lettuce leaves

STIR chopped mint, curry powder, chilli, lime or lemon juice and Thai sweet chilli sauce into the mayonnaise. Add prawns and chill in fridge until ready to serve (up to 24 hours).

TOSS avocado and papaya or melon through prawn mixture. Season with salt and pepper. Serve in beakers or in a basket of rocket or soft lettuce leaves.

Cook's note: For a buffet, toss papaya and avocado with half the lime or lemon juice. Mix remaining juice with curry powder, chilli sauce, mayonnaise and prawns. Season with salt and pepper. Scatter a bed of rocket or soft lettuce leaves on a large serving plate. Top with papaya, avocado and curry prawns.

curried egg sandwiches

• Prepare: 15 minutes • Makes 6-7 sandwiches

Simple and delicious. I've used a ciabatta loaf to make these sandwiches, but they are just as good with thinly sliced brown bread. They can be prepared up to 4 hours in advance, covered with plastic wrap or a damp cloth and kept in a cool place. Great for a picnic.

> 3 hard-boiled eggs, peeled and mashed with a fork
>
> 1 tsp curry powder
>
> 2 tbsp homemade or good-quality mayonnaise (try Best Foods)
>
> 1 tbsp finely chopped coriander or parsley
>
> salt and freshly ground black pepper
>
> handful watercress or rocket leaves
>
> 1 small ciabatta loaf cut into 12-14 thin slices, lightly buttered if desired

COMBINE all filling ingredients except watercress or rocket. Sandwich with leaves between bread. (If using sliced brown bread, remove crusts and cut sandwiches into triangles.)

Cook's note: You can use 2 tbsp soft butter instead of mayonnaise if preferred.

papaya, avocado and prawn salad with curry mayo at top; fresh green chillies below

CHILLI
(capsicum frutescens)

The fire-power of chillies comes from the alkaloid capsaicin, found throughout the fruit, but concentrated in the white membranes which surround the seeds. Wear gloves when working with extra-hot chillies as they can burn the skin. Yoghurt is the best foil to cool a chilli's heat. Fresh chillies can be dried or frozen.

Chilli – the fire wither

The after-effects of a hot chilli are worth the runny nose, the tears, the sweat and the sheer pain! This powerful irritant speeds up the body's metabolism and the shock effect sets off the production of endorphins – those happy hormones which induce a state of euphoria, normally only achieved after strenuous exercise.

AVOCADO
(persea americana)

Throughout the Pacific, where butter exists only as ghee in cans, the avocado is used as a creamy spread. Avocado is one of the few fruits that is rich in fats – albeit, unsaturated and cholesterol-free.

Along with a number of other tropical and sub-tropical fruits, such as mango, papaya, banana, cherimoya, guava, kiwifruit and passionfruit, avocados continue to ripen once picked. Like all tropical fruit, they are best ripened in a warm environment.

The fruit is ripe when it 'gives' slightly when gently squeezed; over-ripe fruit is soft with mushy – often browned – flesh which has an unpleasant aroma and flavour.

Avocado flesh browns quickly when cut. This can be slowed with a splash of lemon juice or other acids such as wine vinegar, and covering tightly to reduce oxidation.

grilled chicken salad with avocado, bacon and bananas

- Prepare: 15 minutes, plus standing
- Cook: 10-15 minutes • Serves 6-8

This salad of crispy noodles, grilled chicken, avocados and bananas tossed in a lemony dressing is a cinch to make and is always popular. The ingredients can be prepared ahead of time, ready for a quick last-minute assembly, but don't slice the avocados or bananas until you're ready to serve to prevent browning.

> 2 tbsp lemon juice
>
> 8 boneless chicken thighs or breasts
>
> 4 rashers bacon
>
> salt and freshly ground black pepper
>
> Pesto Dressing: 2 tbsp Mint and Ginger Pesto✿ or Chilli Coriander Pesto✿; 4 tbsp lemon juice; 2 tbsp flavourless oil (eg. grapeseed)
>
> 1 crunchy lettuce, leaves broken into small pieces
>
> 2 firm avocados
>
> 2 large firm bananas
>
> 2 spring onions, finely sliced
>
> about 6 handfuls crispy noodles

MIX lemon juice through chicken and chill for at least 1 hour (up to 48). While chicken stands, cook bacon until crisp, then dice and set aside.

HEAT grill. Season chicken with salt and pepper and grill for about 15 minutes until cooked through. Stand 5-10 minutes and then slice thinly (remove skin if preferred). Combine dressing ingredients and stir through chicken.

PLACE salad leaves and chicken in a mixing bowl and gently toss. Peel and slice avocados and bananas and gently mix through salad along with spring onions, noodles and bacon. Pile onto a serving plate and serve immediately.

duck and mango rolls

• Prepare: 10 minutes • Makes 8 rolls

Cooked chicken or pork can also be used in place of roasted duck. Serve rolls with oyster sauce.

> shredded flesh $1/2$ roasted Chinese duck (see pg 132), fat and bones removed
>
> 1 tbsp oyster sauce (see pg 130), or sauce from duck
>
> 8 rounds rice paper
>
> flesh 2 mangos, or 1 x 425g (15oz) can mangos in natural juice (drained), sliced into finger-sized strips
>
> 4 spring onions, cut in long thin slices
>
> bunch watercress or rocket, stems removed

COMBINE duck and oyster sauce.

WET a clean teatowel, squeeze out excess water and place on a clean bench. Dunk each piece of rice paper into hot water, count to two then remove and lay on damp towel. After about a minute, the rice paper will soften to a workable texture.

FOLD over the top $1/3$ of each piece of rice paper and flatten. With the folded edge of the wrapper at the top, lay a handful of duck in a vertical band $2/3$ the length of the wrapper, allowing it to extend a little out the top. Add slices of mango, spring onions and a few watercress or rocket leaves – again allowing ends to extend beyond the paper. Fold up the paper at the bottom to enclose filling at the base, then roll up as tightly as you can from left to right.

COVER prepared rolls with damp paper towels, then tightly with plastic wrap. Chill until ready to serve.

Cook's note: Rice paper takes a little practice to get used to handling it – too little water and it won't roll; too much and it falls apart. Try a few sheets before you assemble these rolls.

smoked fish tarts

• Prepare: 20 minutes • Cook: 20 minutes
• Makes 8 individual or 2 large tarts

These tarts combine appealing textures of flavoursome smoked fish, crisp watercress and crunchy pastry. Great for a lunch party or light supper. Everything can be prepared ahead of time, ready for a quick last-minute assembly.

> Easy Savoury Shortcrust Pastry: 2 cups high-grade flour; pinch salt; 150g (5oz) cold butter, diced; $1/4$ cup cold water
>
> 500g (1lb) smoked fish, flaked with no bones
>
> 1 cup Lime Mayonnaise✪ or Wasabi Lime Mayonnaise✪
>
> 2 double kaffir lime leaves, finely shredded
>
> $1/2$ telegraph cucumber, chopped in very small dice
>
> several handfuls fresh watercress tips or baby spinach leaves
>
> spring onion, finely shredded

PROCESS or rub in flour, salt and butter until mixture forms fine crumbs. Mix in cold water to make a softish dough.

ROLL out pastry thinly and press into 8 individual shallow tart pans. (Alternatively, roll pastry to fit 2 x 23cm/9in shallow pie tins.) Chill for at least 10 minutes or until ready to cook.

HEAT oven to 220°C (425°F/gas 7). Bake pastry for 5 minutes then reduce heat to 180°C (350°F/gas 4) and bake a further 15-20 minutes until crisp and golden. Put to one side to cool.

COMBINE fish, mayonnaise, kaffir lime leaves and cucumber (reserve a little for garnish) in a mixing bowl. Divide filling over cooked tart bases. Top with watercress or spinach leaves and spring onion. Sprinkle with extra cucumber.

Cook's note: Cooked pastry shells will keep fresh in a sealed container for a few days or can be frozen. Refresh in a hot oven for a few minutes if they soften.

**duck and mango rolls
served with oyster sauce**

A SORCERER'S DIET

Sorcerers and wizards wielded
immense power in early Pacific
societies. Even today, a curious
blend of Christianity and
'heathen' custom survives.
William Wyatt Gill, who spent most
of his adult life in the Cook Islands,
recounts in his book
Cook Islands Customs, the story of
a conversation he had in 1892 with
Taraaere, the last priest of Tangarao
(who had offered human sacrifices
to the protective god of
Rarotonga), when he Taraaere was
nearly 90: "My father taught me
how to retain wisdom (korero);
he also told me when to marry.
He did not feed me with plantains,
bananas and fish, lest, the food
being slippery and light, wisdom
should slip away from me. No!
He fed me with taro, well beaten
with a pestle and mixed with
cooked taro leaves – the glutinous
nature of taro being favourable
to the retention of memory."
It would seem that the priests and
wizards of such times all followed
Taraaere's regime. If nothing else
it certainly promoted
impressive longevity.

fijian chicken curry

- Prepare: 10 minutes • Cook: 15 minutes
- Serves 4

The Indian curries found in Fiji tend to use an aromatic mixture of spices and water, rather than coconut milk.

1 tbsp each coriander seeds, cumin seeds and black mustard seeds

3 tbsp flavourless oil (eg. grapeseed)

1 large onion, peeled and finely diced

2 tbsp curry powder

2 tbsp minced fresh ginger

5 cloves garlic, peeled and crushed

400g (14oz) thinly sliced boneless, skinless chicken

handful snake beans or green beans, cut into 4cm (1$^1/_2$) lengths

2 cups water

salt and freshly ground black pepper

TOAST spices in a dry frypan until they start to smell fragrant (do not burn). Grind coarsely.

HEAT oil in pan and gently cook onion, curry powder, ginger and garlic with ground spices for about 5 minutes until onion has softened.

ADD chicken, beans and water. Season, cover tightly and simmer for about 10 minutes, stirring occasionally. (Add more water if needed, until the sauce reaches a light coating consistency.)

Cook's notes:
- If using lamb or goat for this curry, choose a lean cut, such as leg steak or loin, and slice thinly across the grain. The cooking time will be about the same as for chicken.
- Black mustard seeds are hotter than the yellow variety (which can be substituted). Use in pickling mixtures and to flavour fried dishes.
- Snake beans, which thrive in tropical climates, are very long and thin. Choose crisp, dark-green and blemish-free beans and cook in the same way as regular beans.

spicy pork meatloaf

- Prepare: 5 minutes • Cook: 50-60 minutes
- Serves 6-8

Use fresh mince for this loaf, as the liquid exuded from thawed, frozen meats makes it sloppy. It's a great loaf for picnics and summer lunches. Here, I've served it cold with Red Onion, Pineapple and Watercress Salad✤, but you could also try it hot with Sweet Potato Mash✤ and Cashew and Mustard Salsa✤.

1 cup fresh breadcrumbs

$^1/_4$ cup milk

2 spring onions, roughly chopped

4 cloves garlic, peeled

4cm (1$^1/_2$in) piece fresh ginger, peeled

2 tsp finely grated lime or lemon rind (no pith)

$^1/_4$ cup fresh coriander, chopped

2 tbsp fish sauce

$^1/_2$ tsp salt

1 egg white

1kg (2$^1/_4$lb) fresh lean pork or beef mince

2 tbsp Thai sweet chilli sauce, plus extra for serving

HEAT oven to 180°C (350°F/gas 4). Grease or line a baking tray. Soak bread in milk.

PUREE together spring onions, garlic, ginger, lime or lemon rind, coriander, fish sauce, salt and egg white until smooth. Add soaked bread.

COMBINE bread mixture with mince. Press firmly into a 20cm x 12cm (8in x 4$^1/_2$in) loaf tin. Unmould onto prepared tray. Brush top with chilli sauce and bake in oven for 50-60 minutes or until juices run clear when pricked and loaf feels bouncy when pressed.

COOL and chill for at least 2 hours. When cold, slice and serve with extra Thai sweet chilli sauce.

Cook's note: The meatloaf will keep in the fridge for 3-4 days. The raw mixture can also be used to make meatballs or barbecue patties.

spicy dhal

- Prepare: 10 minutes, plus standing
- Cook: 15-20 minutes • Makes about 3 cups (serves 4)

Fiji is a great place to eat Indian food. Hundreds of hole-in-the-wall cafés serve simple, fresh meals for a few dollars. While dhal is usually served as a side dish to accompany curries, I often serve it for a busy mid-week dinner with röti✿.

1 cup brown lentils

3 cups boiling water

2 tsp each cumin seeds and black mustard seeds (see pg 73)

2 tbsp oil

1 onion, peeled and finely chopped

1 tbsp minced fresh ginger

3 cloves garlic, peeled and crushed

1 tbsp curry powder

2 cups hot water

1 x 400g (14oz) can chopped tomatoes in juice

1 cinnamon stick

5 each whole cloves and whole cardamoms

salt and freshly ground black pepper

$1/4$ cup chopped fresh coriander

COVER lentils with boiling water and stand for 10 minutes. Drain.

PLACE cumin and mustard seeds in a hot dry frypan and toast for a couple of minutes (don't burn; they should just start to release their aromas). Remove from pan and grind.

ADD oil to pan and gently cook onion, ginger and garlic with ground spices and curry powder for about 5 minutes. Add lentils, hot water, tomatoes, cinnamon stick, cloves and cardamoms. Simmer for 10-15 minutes, uncovered, until liquid has been absorbed and lentils are tender but not mushy. Season to taste with salt and lots of black pepper and add fresh coriander at the last minute.

BREADFRUIT
(artocarpus altilis)

This Pacific native thrives even on coral atolls and is an important staple for Polynesians, Melanesians and Micronesians. The fruit comes into season primarily over the summer months and has a spongy eggplant-like texture when raw. In many island cultures, the fruit is roasted in a fire, then peeled and pounded or rolled until it acquires a dough-like consistency. Served in thin slabs with fresh coconut milk, it is a satisfying – though not particularly nutritious – starch.

röti

• Prepare: 15 minutes, plus standing
• Cook: 4 minutes (per röti) • Makes 10

This simple flatbread is quick to prepare and requires no special equipment. A short rest of the prepared dough allows the gluten to 'relax', making it easy to roll out thinly.

2 cups high-grade flour, plus extra for kneading

1 cup water

2 tbsp soft butter

2 tsp cumin seeds, toasted and ground

1 tsp salt

PUT flour into mixing bowl. Make a well in the middle, pour in water and mix to a smooth dough. Turn out onto a lightly floured board and knead a few times. Put dough back into bowl to 'rest' for at least 10 minutes (or covered for up to 12 hours).

DIVIDE dough into 10 pieces and roll out each on a lightly floured board into a flat disc roughly 14cm (5½in) in diameter. Rub a little butter over each disc and sprinkle lightly with combined ground cumin and salt.

ROLL-UP discs into a cigar shape then form each into a tight, round coil. Place on a lightly floured tray until ready to cook. (They can be prepared to this point and chilled for up to 4 hours.)

ROLL out each coil as thinly as possible on a lightly floured surface. Heat a heavy, dry frypan and cook röti, one at a time, over medium-high heat for about 2 minutes on each side. Fold in half and stack on a plate.

Cook's notes:
• You can use other spices instead of cumin, or leave out altogether and just use salt.
• Röti are best eaten fresh, though they can be reheated. Wrap in foil and place in a hot oven for a few minutes.

spicy dhal and röti at top.
beating cooked breadfruit below

The early Polynesians were talented mariners well-versed in the skills of celestial navigation. More than 3000 years ago, travelling in the fastest vessels the world had ever known – double-hulled craft capable of bursts of speed up to 30 knots – they moved freely from island to island. Their annual calendar was measured in the signs of nature – the migration of birds, the spawning of fish and fruiting of crops. In Samoa and Tonga, a little worm,

palolo, comes up from the reef in April and May and later in the year in October and November. Today, the locals paddle out onto the reef and scoop up this delicacy, eating it raw or frying it in batter. In addition to being the name of the worm, the term 'palolo' is used to describe the time of year. Further east, there are no worms, but the word is still used to describe the season.

harvests from the sea

Fishing is in the blood of these seafaring islanders. For centuries, they have skilfully navigated the vast wilderness of the Pacific, reading the moods of the sea and the lie of stars in the heavens; gauging sky and wind before heading out through the reef to deep open water in search of the big game fish – mahi mahi, wahoo, tuna, marlin, flying fish, kingfish and mackerel.

Inside, or on the edge of the reef, men wait for the tide to net and spear parrot fish, trevally, drummer and unicorn fish.

The women work the shallows, searching rocky hollows for octopus, wading the reef for shellfish, prickly kina (sea urchins) and sea slugs. Their harvests will be eaten raw, cured in lime juice with a sauce of coconut milk, or cooked in an earth oven or over a fire. Leftovers are smoked, dried or 'cured'. Nothing will be wasted – who knows what tomorrow will bring.

crayfish salad with asian seafood dressing

• Prepare: 15 minutes • Serves 6

The components for this luxurious salad can be prepared ahead of time ready for a quick, last-minute assembly. I have served it with an Asian Seafood Dressing, but Lime Mayonnaise✿ is a good alternative.

1 whole butterhead lettuce, leaves separated, washed and dried

about 18 asparagus spears, lightly cooked, cooled and drained

about 18 snowpeas, dunked in boiling water then cooled under cold water, drained

2 just-ripe avocados, peeled and cut in wedges

2-3 cooked crayfish tails, gut removed, flesh sliced into thin medallions

Asian Seafood Dressing: 1 tsp sesame oil, 1 tsp light soy sauce, 2 tsp fish sauce, 2 tbsp lime juice, $1/2$ tsp brown sugar

1 tbsp toasted sesame seeds

PREPARE all salad ingredients for assembly and chill. Combine dressing ingredients.

ASSEMBLE salad by placing a few lettuce leaves on each plate. Divide over asparagus, snowpeas, avocado and crayfish. Drizzle with dressing. Sprinkle each salad with a few sesame seeds and serve at once.

Variation: Use crabmeat, prawns or cooked boneless chunks of fish in place of crayfish.

crayfish salad with asian seafood dressing at top, tropical lobster below

steamed baby paua with asian flavours

- Prepare: 10 minutes • Cook: 2-3 minutes
- Serves 6-8 as an appetiser

Abalone, known as paua by the Maori of New Zealand, grow prolifically in the southern waters of New Zealand, the Chatham Islands and Australia. They are now farmed, taking around 18 months to reach cocktail size, which – unlike the large, wild variety – don't need pulverising to tenderise.

> 2 tbsp finely shredded fresh ginger
>
> ¹/₂ leek (green part only) cut into thin matchstick strips
>
> 18 farmed baby paua
>
> Dressing: 1 tsp sesame oil, 2 tbsp oyster sauce (see pg 130), 1 tbsp sake or rice wine

POUR boiling water over ginger and leeks. Stand 1 minute then cool under cold water. Drain well.

REMOVE each paua from its shell, discarding gut sac (paua aficionados may prefer to leave it on as it is much milder than the sac of a full-grown paua). Return pauas to shells and top each with a little ginger and leek.

MIX dressing ingredients together. Spoon about ¹/₂ tsp onto each paua. Place in a steamer, cover and cook for 2-3 minutes until just tender (do not overcook).

Cook's note: Sake, a brewed alcoholic drink, is important in the Japanese kitchen, where it is used to tenderise, tone down saltiness, remove strong smells and fishy odours, and to preserve delicate flavours. Mirin (rice wine) is milder but can be used as a substitute.

steamed baby paua with asian flavours at top. fishing the lagoon below

FOR SEA SLUGS

... are out on the reef
... ic buckets and a knife
... llecting seafood.
Her small son hovers like a bird
for the morsels his mother
extracts from the shells.
She grasps a slimy green sea
slug and with a quick flick of
her knife slits it across the
middle – squeezing it to reveal
the reddish innards.
"Not ready," she says, chucking
the creature back into the water –
where it will recover. "Needs to
look like white spaghetti."
She waves her screwdriver
under my nose, then passes me
another morsel of shellfish:
"Torokai," she says. "Delicious."
It is – chewy, but good.
She grabs a grey slug, beats it
against her leg a few times,
roughly scrapes it and cuts me
a slice. "Ngata," she announces
with pleasure. At first bite,
it seems crisply appealing,
but within seconds it
disintegrates into a disgusting,
jelly slime. She notes my
grimace with a smile:
"Gotta eat that one fast!"

Rarotonga, April 1999

grilled crayfish with saffron lime butter

- **Prepare**: 5 minutes • **Cook**: 6-8 minutes
- **Serves 6 as a first course**

Crayfish or lobster can be used for this wonderful dish. The sweet, rich flavour of the flesh can be lost in boiling, but is retained when grilled. If preferred, plain butter, or any other flavoured butter (see *Variation*, below), can be used to baste the crayfish. The most acceptable way to dispatch a live cray is to cut through the head between the eyes with a heavy, sharp knife, which kills the fish instantly, or place in the freezer for an hour or two.

Saffron Lime Butter: 80-100g (3-4oz) butter, softened; finely grated rind 1 lime (no pith), plus 2 tbsp lime juice; 1 spring onion, finely sliced; 2 double kaffir lime leaves, finely sliced (optional); 20 saffron threads, crushed

3 crayfish tails, split in half, gut thread removed and discarded

salt and freshly ground black pepper

MIX butter with lime rind and juice, spring onion, kaffir lime leaves and saffron threads.

HEAT grill. Season each cray tail with a little salt and pepper. Spread about 1 tbsp of the saffron butter over each tail. Place under hot grill and cook for 6-8 minutes until flesh is no longer opaque and is springy to the touch.

Variation: To make a Sesame and Ginger Butter, mix 50g (2oz) softened butter with 2 tbsp minced fresh ginger, 2 tsp sesame oil and 1 finely minced spring onion.

seared tuna steak on chinese radish salad

- Prepare: 10 minutes, plus standing
- Cook: less than 1 minute
- Serves 6 as a first course

This stylish treatment for tuna, inspired by chef Peter Chichester, gives a melt-in-the-mouth result and can be prepared ahead of time. The tuna needs to be really fresh. Remove the small nub on the side that contains white connective tissue. (If you leave it on, the tuna tears when you slice it.)

350g (12oz) piece tuna loin, trimmed

1 tsp sesame oil

1 tbsp black peppercorns

1 tsp ground chilli

salt

Chinese Radish Salad: 2 cups shredded Japanese radish; 1 small carrot, peeled and shredded; 1 bunch spinach leaves, shredded (optional); 2 tbsp chopped coriander; 100g (4oz) pickled ginger (see pg 106), shredded; $1/2$ telegraph cucumber, shredded

Sake Dressing: 1 tbsp sesame oil; 2 tbsp flavourless oil (eg, grapeseed); 1 tbsp shoyu or light soy; 2 tbsp sake; 1 tbsp lemon juice; 1 tbsp rice wine vinegar

RUB tuna with sesame oil. Grind over peppercorns and rub into flesh with chilli. Season with salt. Heat a hot-plate or heavy frypan. When very hot, lightly oil and sear tuna for 15 seconds on each side. Transfer to a dish filled with ice or pack with frozen freezer pads. Cool for 10 minutes, remove and chill for at least 1 hour (up to 24).

COMBINE salad ingredients. Whisk dressing ingredients and keep at room temperature. At serving time, toss dressing through salad.

ARRANGE salad on plates. With a sharp knife, use a sawing motion to cut thin slices of tuna and arrange over salads. Serve at once.

prawns with chilli mango sauce

- Prepare: 10 minutes • Cook: 5 minutes • Serves 4

The sweet, fruity flavour of mangos, coupled with fiery chillies and aromatic spices, makes a perfect partner for prawns and fish. This wonderful sauce also makes a great accompaniment to barbecued seafood. Serve on a bed of rice or crispy noodles.

Chilli Mango Sauce: 1 ripe mango, peeled and flesh chopped; 1 fresh red chilli, deseeded, pith removed and chopped; 1-2 tsp (to taste) Tabasco or other hot pepper sauce; 2 large cloves garlic, peeled and chopped; 1 tbsp finely chopped ginger; $1/4$ cup desiccated coconut (see pg 146); $1/2$ tsp each ground coriander and cumin; $1/2$ cup coconut cream; $1/4$ cup lemon juice; 3 tbsp chopped fresh coriander leaves, salt and freshly ground black pepper

2 tbsp peanut oil

1 each red and yellow pepper, deseeded, pith removed and finely chopped

24-30 large raw prawns, peeled and deveined

PUREE all the sauce ingredients. Transfer to a pot and simmer for 3 minutes.

HEAT peanut oil in a large frypan or pot and cook the peppers for 2-3 minutes until their colour changes. Add the mango sauce and bring to a simmer.

MIX in the prawns and cook for about 2 minutes, stirring frequently, until prawns change colour (do not overcook). Serve straightaway.

Cook's note: Prepared sauce will keep in the fridge for several days.

seared tuna steak on chinese radish salad at top, prawns with chilli mango sauce below

TARO
(arum species)

Taro is the most important common food of the Pacific, eaten both in everyday meals and ceremonial feasts. So many species and varieties in the tuber-producing *arum* family come under the name of taro, that botanists have found it a nightmare to classify. Shaggy-topped, barrel-shaped taro tubers have a gluey, starchy texture, bland flavour and pale, purplish-grey flesh when cooked. Both the leaves and the tubers must be thoroughly cooked to eliminate their oxalic acid, which is an unpleasant irritant to throat and mouth. Use a little oil on your hands when peeling the tubers to prevent skin irritations. The flesh holds texture and shape when boiled or steamed and soaks up flavours well in soups and stews. Baked taro tends to be quite dry, but it roasts and fries well. Young taro leaves are delicious cooked in coconut cream for the classic Pacific dish Palusami (see pg 132), and cooked leaves can be used as a substitute for spinach.

ROTTEN FOOD

While Rarotongans consider partially rotted raw sea slugs a delicacy (they leave them in a soft-drink bottle for a few days to 'mature'), and the Samoans ferment breadfruit – the older the better – the penchant for strongly flavoured, even partly rotten food, is most evident in early Maori culture. Originally a necessity – constant warring between tribes left little time for cultivation, and crops often rotted before they could be harvested – Maori eventually developed a taste for rotten food. Even today, corn, potatoes, sea urchins and crayfish are still commonly enjoyed this way. Kaanga wai is prepared by soaking corn cobs in fresh running water for 2-3 months until the core is rotten. The corn is then stripped from the husk and cooked into a kind of porridge. The smell is foul but the taste, once you get it past your nose, is surprisingly sweet and nutty. Today, pottles of kaanga wai (or kaanga pirau, as it is sometimes called), can be bought at the Saturday Market in Otara, Auckland, the largest Polynesian market in the world.

salad of chargrilled squid on soba noodles

- Prepare: 15 minutes, plus marinating
- Cook: 6-10 minutes • Serves 4

Any kind of seafood, or even grilled chicken, can be served on this terrific Soba-noodle Salad. Grilled squid cooks in a flash and makes an appealing texture combination with the noodles.

> 400g (14oz) cleaned squid
>
> 2 tbsp flavourless oil (eg. grapeseed)
>
> 1 tsp sesame oil
>
> 2 cloves garlic, peeled and crushed
>
> 1 tsp minced fresh ginger
>
> 1 small red chilli, deseeded, pith removed and minced
>
> Dressing: 2 tbsp lime or lemon juice; 2 tbsp flavourless oil (eg. grapeseed); 1 tbsp soy sauce; 1 tbsp fish sauce; 1 tsp brown sugar; 1 tomato, chopped
>
> Soba-noodle Salad: 250g (9oz) dry soba noodles; 1 tomato, finely chopped; 1 spring onion, finely sliced; 2 tbsp chopped coriander; salt

CLEAN the squid and cut into 5cm (2in) pieces (if using baby squid, cut bodies in half).

MIX squid pieces in a bowl with oils, garlic, ginger and chilli. Chill for 30 minutes.

PUREE dressing ingredients until smooth.

COOK noodles according to packet directions. Cool under cold water, drain thoroughly and toss with half of the dressing mixture, the tomato, spring onion and coriander. Season to taste. Pile onto a large flat plate or chill until ready to serve. (Salad can be prepared to this point a few hours ahead of time.)

HEAT barbecue hot-plate. Cook squid for 1-2 minutes until lightly charred and opaque. Mix rest of dressing through squid and pile on top of noodles.

grilled spicy fish cakes wrapped in banana leaves

- Prepare: 15 minutes • Cook: 6 minutes
- Makes 12-14 (serve 1-2 per person)

Use foil or baking paper if you can't find fresh banana leaves. If they are available, cut into squares on either side of the backbone. If the leaves won't fold easily, pass over an open flame to soften. The fish-cake mixture is also yummy cooked plain, without the wrappers, as little patties. Serve with Chilli Lime Dipping Sauce✿.

> 1 spring onion, chopped
>
> 1 red chilli, deseeded, pith removed and chopped
>
> finely grated rind 1 lime or lemon (no pith)
>
> 2 tsp minced fresh ginger
>
> 1 tbsp fish sauce
>
> $1/4$ cup chopped coriander or mint leaves
>
> 300g (11oz) boneless white fish, chopped
>
> 12-14 pieces fresh banana leaf (12-15cm/5-6in squares)

PUREE all ingredients, except fish and banana leaves, to a paste. Add fish; blend until smooth.

PLACE a tablespoon of mixture onto each leaf. Fold to enclose filling; secure with a toothpick.

HEAT barbecue or grill and cook parcels for 3 minutes each side until they feel springy – the outsides will be slightly charred. Remove and discard wrappers before eating. (To cook as patties, cook spoonfuls of the mixture on a lightly oiled barbecue hot-plate.)

Cook's note: If doubling or trebling recipe for a group, cook mixture as patties then wrap in banana leaves and chill. When ready to serve, cook parcels on barbecue for about 1 minute on each side to heat through.

cardamom and coriander spiced fish sticks

• Prepare: 10 minutes, plus marinating
• Cook: 4-5 minutes • Makes 12 (serves 4-6)

The combination of lime, coriander, garlic and cardamom works especially well with fish. (Try the marinade also on fish fillets, flash-roasted in a very hot oven for 5-6 minutes.) If you can, use whole coriander plants, including the stems and roots, as their flavour is excellent. Here, I've served the fish sticks with Fried Plantain, Cashews and Coconut✿.

2 whole coriander plants, washed and chopped (about ¹/₂ cup, tightly packed)

finely grated rind (no pith) and juice 1 lime

2 cloves garlic, peeled and crushed

1 tsp cardamom seeds, crushed

1 tsp minced fresh ginger

2 tbsp flavourless oil (eg. grapeseed)

salt and freshly ground black pepper

500-600g (1¹/₄lb) fresh, dense, white fish fillets, cut into longish strips 2-3cm (1in) wide

1 cup plain yoghurt

PUREE all ingredients, except fish and yoghurt, to a smoothish paste. Mix half of the mixture through fish and chill for up to 4 hours. Set aside remaining marinade.

HEAT a lightly oiled barbecue or grill. Shake excess marinade off fish and thread fish onto about 12 bamboo skewers and spray with oil. Cook fish sticks over high heat for about 2 minutes each side until cooked through. (Run a fish slice under the sticks before turning over to prevent them sticking.)

MIX reserved marinade with plain yoghurt, check seasoning and serve with sticks.

grilled scallop salad with citrus chilli dressing

• Prepare: 15 minutes • Cook: 1-2 minutes
• Serves 6

The divine dressing in this salad is best prepared at least 12 hours in advance. It's wonderful on all types of seafood, as well as chicken and meat.

Citrus Chilli Dressing: juice 1 orange; juice 2 limes or lemons; 3 tbsp rice wine vinegar; 2 tbsp fish sauce; 1 tsp minced fresh ginger; ¹/₂ tsp hot chilli sauce; 1 clove garlic, peeled and crushed; 1 tbsp sugar; salt and freshly ground black pepper

1 tbsp flavourless oil (eg. grapeseed)

500g (1lb) fresh scallops

salt and freshly ground black pepper

2 tbsp each finely chopped coriander and mint

8 handfuls mixed salad greens

¹/₂ red onion, peeled and finely chopped

3 oranges, peeled and segmented

1 large avocado, peeled and cut into wedges

COMBINE all dressing ingredients and chill in the fridge until ready to use.

HEAT a barbecue hot-plate or frypan. Mix oil through scallops and season with salt and pepper. Briefly cook for about a minute (do not overcook). If cooking in a frypan, add the cooking juices to the dressing.

MIX coriander and mint into dressing. Drizzle a little dressing over the salad greens and toss to coat. Gently toss through red onion, orange segments and avocado. Divide greens between plates and top with scallops. Spoon over remaining dressing.

Cook's note: Stored in a sealed jar, the Citrus Chilli Dressing will keep in the fridge for up to a week.

fresh ginger, Santo Island Markets, at top; cardamom and coriander spiced fish sticks served with fried plantain, cashews and coconut below

GINGER
(zingiber officinale)

Throughout history, ginger has played a key role both as a spice and a medicine. As well as acting as a general restorative, health benefits include relieving unsettled stomachs, nausea, menstrual cramps and colds. In the kitchen, ginger imparts a cleansing spicy flavour, counter-balances fatty flavours in pork and duck and takes away the fishy smell from seafood.

Ginger – a refreshing curative

Fresh or young ginger has a thin skin, is very mild and juicy and perishes quickly. Use it as a vegetable or for pickling. Mature ginger has a firmer golden skin, fibrous texture and a stronger flavour. Peel before grating or mincing. Store ginger rhizomes in the fridge for a couple of weeks wrapped in a paper towel, freeze or place in vinegar or sherry.

kokoda – coconut ceviche

- Prepare: 10 minutes, plus standing
- Serves 4 as a first course

Raw fish marinated in lime juice and mixed with coconut cream is a traditional Pacific-Island favourite, known as kokoda or, in the Cook Islands, ika mata. Fresh tuna is the local fish of choice for this easy, cold fish salad, but any very fresh fish can be used.

> 400g (14oz) freshest tuna
> $1/2$ cup lime or lemon juice
> $1/4$ cup thick coconut cream
> $1/4$ red onion, peeled and cut in very thin strips
> handful chopped coriander
> 1 spring onion, finely sliced
> 1 green or red chilli, deseeded, pith removed and minced
> salt and freshly ground black pepper

CUT tuna into thin strips or small dice. Mix through lime or lemon juice and leave for at least 1 hour – or up to 4 – in the fridge. (The more finely sliced the fish, the quicker it will 'cook' in the citrus juice.)

COMBINE remaining ingredients. Drain tuna, discarding juice, and toss through coconut mixture. Adjust seasoning and serve at once.

Variations:
- Coconut Crab Ceviche – use same weight of fresh, cooked or raw crab meat in place of fish, squeezing out excess moisture before marinating in the lime juice.
- Scallop Ceviche – use fresh scallops and slice in half through the middle before marinating in lime juice.

scallops barbecued with chilli lime coconut sauce

- Prepare: 5 minutes • Cook: 15 minutes • Serves 4

In this recipe, the flavours of lime, kaffir lime and chilli combine with coconut cream for a rich tangy sauce. If you prefer, you can use 3-4 tbsp butter instead of coconut cream to get a richly flavoured piquant butter in which to cook the seafood. For this recipe, I like to keep the orange roes on the scallops. Serve with Coconut Rice○.

> Chilli Lime Coconut Sauce: finely grated rind 1 lime (no pith), plus 1 tbsp lime juice; 1 tsp minced fresh red chilli; 2 double kaffir lime leaves, finely shredded (or rind 2 extra limes); 1 cup coconut cream; pinch each salt and sugar; freshly ground black pepper
> 20 scallops
> salt and freshly ground black pepper
> 2 tbsp butter
> 1 spring onion, finely shredded

COMBINE sauce ingredients in a small pot. Heat for at least 10-15 minutes to a creamy consistency.

SEASON scallops with salt and pepper. Heat a barbecue hot-plate or heavy frypan. When hot, add butter and, when it starts to brown, cook scallops and spring onions for 2 minutes until scallops are just cooked.

ADD scallops to coconut sauce, warm through gently and serve at once.

Cook's note: Scallops can also be threaded onto soaked bamboo skewers, seasoned, then barbecued and served drizzled with sauce. Take care not to over-cook the scallops – use a high heat and cook just prior to serving.

prawns in singapore chilli sauce

- Prepare: 10 minutes • Cook: 15 minutes
- Serves 4

This delicious sauce, traditionally used to make Singapore Chilli Crab, is very useful for all kinds of seafood. Here, I've used prawns, but it's also yummy with fresh fish. Serve on a bed of rice.

Singapore Chilli Sauce: 2 tbsp flavourless oil (eg, grapeseed); 1 tbsp minced fresh ginger; 1 tsp crushed garlic; 3 fresh red chillies, deseeded, pith removed and chopped; 2 tbsp tomato ketchup; $\frac{1}{4}$ cup Thai sweet chilli sauce; 1 tbsp brown sugar; 2 tbsp light soy sauce; 1 tbsp fish sauce

flavourless oil (eg, grapeseed) for frying

500g (1lb) fresh green prawns or prawn tails, or 4 fresh, boneless, white fish fillets (eg, snapper, terikihi, blue cod)

Garnish (optional): green papaya or mango, peeled and grated; 1 tbsp chopped coriander

MAKE sauce by heating oil and gently frying ginger, garlic and chillies for a couple of minutes. Mix in remaining sauce ingredients and simmer for 5 minutes.

HEAT oil in a frypan and add prawns or fish. Fry quickly on both sides, then pour sauce over seafood. Stir once (be careful if using fish not to break it up) and allow to simmer for a couple of minutes until prawns are pink or fish is cooked through. Garnish with grated green papaya or mango mixed with coriander.

Cook's notes:
- The prepared sauce will keep in the fridge for up to a week.
- Green papaya can be cooked as a vegetable either in curries or soups, where it will retain its texture. It is also used to make pickles or can be grated raw for salads.

92

CELEBRATION LUNCH

- smoked fish tarts
- seared sesame salmon with udon noodles
- duck and mango salad
- lime soufflés

lime and coriander flash-roasted fish

• Prepare: 5 minutes • Cook: 6-8 minutes
• Serves 6

One of my favourite ways to cook fresh fish fillets is by roasting them quickly in a hot oven. They taste really good served with Lemongrass and Chilli Risotto°. To get the timing right, heat the oven when you put the risotto on to cook, and cook the fish during the last 5 minutes of the risotto's cooking time.

6 very fresh, boneless, fish fillets

1 tsp minced red chilli

finely grated rind 1 lime (no pith),
plus 2 tbsp juice

1 tsp sugar

salt and freshly ground black pepper

$1/4$ cup chopped fresh coriander

HEAT oven to 240°C (475°F/gas 9) and line a shallow tray with baking paper.

ARRANGE fish on prepared tray, leaving a little space between pieces. Combine chilli, lime rind, juice and sugar, and spread over fillets. Season with salt and pepper and sprinkle with coriander.

COOK for 6-8 minutes until flesh is opaque and fish is cooked through. Stand for 2 minutes before serving.

pipis with coconut sauce

• Prepare: 5 minutes • Cook: 5-6 minutes
• Serves 4

Store-cupboard stand-bys of coconut cream, fish sauce and chilli sauce make fast work of this flavoursome sauce. It's a great treatment for pipis and other shellfish.

1 tsp grated palm sugar (see pg 143)
or brown sugar

1 cup coconut cream

2 tbsp Thai sweet chilli sauce

1 tbsp fish sauce

30-40 live pipis, washed, or mussels, washed and beards removed

2 spring onions, finely chopped

2 tbsp chopped coriander

2 double kaffir lime leaves, finely shredded, or finely grated rind 1 lime (no pith)

PLACE sugar, coconut cream, chilli sauce and fish sauce in a large pot. Bring to a fast boil.

ADD pipis or mussels and spring onions, cover and cook only for as long as it takes for shells to open (discard any that don't). Mix through coriander and shredded kaffir lime leaves or lime rind. Serve shellfish in deep bowls with sauce poured over.

Cook's note: If pipis are sandy, place in a bucket of cold seawater, sprinkle with a little flour or rolled oats and leave in a cool place for 8-12 hours (they will spit out their sand).

Before any indigenous settlement, the islands of the Pacific were dramatically inhospitable. Many had no food, apart from an abundant supply of fish in the seas, and, of the plants that grew naturally, more than nine out of 10 were found nowhere else on earth. Without the benefit of metal or clay, the early Polynesians created settlements of small communities – bartering food, buying wives, sharing ideas and, occasionally, fighting for territory and resources. Quickly, the coconut palm became the staff of life; source of all things

– a quenching drink in times of drought and, from the ripe nut, an essential source of nourishment. The coconut also provided fuel, fibre for matting and materials to build and thatch dwellings, make utensils, serving bowls, storage containers and tools. The manufacture of Tapa cloth from the inner bark of certain trees, especially the paper mulberry is an ancient craft practised throughout the Pacific, from Melanesia through to Hawaii and even New Zealand.

at dusk

whetting the appetite

As the sun sinks in the sky, the women are in the chief's hut preparing lap lap for tonight's meal. One stacks a pile of never (island cabbage) leaves, another works with a bamboo knife – used for everything from cutting soft crops to performing circumcisions – to peel the skin from a thick green banana.

Everyone has a job: grating, peeling, slicing, tending the fire, preparing fresh coconut milk and, finally, wrapping and tying the two big parcels of food for the umu.

Tonight, in our honour, there will be lap lap of chicken and green banana, and lap lap of cabbage leaves, chopped taro, yams and tiny whole reef fish. Each is anointed with coconut cream before being wrapped in layers of banana leaves and covered with hot rocks.

The men sip kava from dried coconut shells. Soon we will be feasting.

KAVA

(piper methysticum)

Ancient voyagers introduced kava from Vanuatu eastwards into the high islands of tropical Polynesia, where it is now widely cultivated. In the general absence of alcohol, kava serves as the opiate of the Pacific. The grated, chewed or dry powdered roots are mixed with water to produce a slightly narcotic drink which is used for both social and ceremonial occasions. Vanuatu grows the Pacific's most potent kava. Over 75 different varieties are cultivated here, including the 'two-dei' kava which is rumoured to be so strong as to induce a two-day sleep after taking it. Kava contains a number of different chemical compounds and sensitises both hearing and sight. Kava is also a useful healing plant for urinary tract and stomach ailments. In the West, it has been popularised as a natural stress remedy.

coconut and coriander fish fritters

- Prepare: 5 minutes, plus standing
- Cook: 4 minutes (per batch)
- Makes about 36 fritters

Fritter batters are simple to prepare and provide the base for all kinds of flavouring combinations – fresh fish, coriander, coconut and banana is one of my favourites. These little fritters are delicious served with a Fresh Mango Salsa○.

> 1 cup self-raising flour
>
> 2 eggs
>
> 1 tsp salt and generous grind freshly ground black pepper
>
> $^1/_2$ cup chilled soda water or cold water
>
> 300g (11oz) fresh, boneless fish, diced into 1-2cm ($^1/_2$in) pieces
>
> $^1/_2$ cup desiccated coconut (see pg 146), lightly toasted
>
> 1 ripe banana, peeled and mashed
>
> $^1/_4$ cup chopped coriander
>
> 2 tbsp Thai sweet chilli sauce
>
> flavourless oil (eg. grapeseed) for frying

MIX flour, eggs, salt, pepper and water to a smooth batter. Mix in all other ingredients, except the oil. Stand for 5-10 minutes before cooking.

HEAT 1cm ($^1/_2$in) oil in a large heavy frypan and, working in batches, cook teaspoonfuls of the mixture over medium heat for about 2 minutes each side until fritters are golden and cooked through.

Cook's note: These fritters can be made ahead of time and reheated in a 200°C (400°F/gas 6) oven for about 5 minutes.

coconut and coriander fish fritters
served with fresh mango salsa

steamed prawn dumplings

- Prepare: 10 minutes • Cook: 5 minutes
- Makes 14 dumplings

Keep a store of wonton wrappers on hand to make these delicate, light dumplings. All kinds of fillings can be used – you'll find a heartier variation using pork mince below.

200g (7oz) green prawns or shrimp meat, roughly chopped

1 tbsp finely sliced spring onion

$1/2$ tsp sesame oil

1 tsp crushed garlic

salt and freshly ground black pepper

14 wonton wrappers (see pg 102)

Tamari Dipping Sauce: half-and-half mix tamari (see pg 102), or light soy, and sake (see pg 81)

MIX prawns or shrimp meat with spring onion, sesame oil and garlic. Season with salt and pepper. Place a teaspoonful of prawn mix on wonton wrappers and squeeze tight around the filling to form a purse with an open top.

COOK in a covered, oiled steamer for 5 minutes, or until springy to the touch. Serve with the dipping sauce.

Variation: For Ginger Pork Dumplings, mix 200g (7oz) fresh pork mince with 1 spring onion, minced; 2 tsp minced fresh ginger; 1 tsp sesame oil; 1 clove garlic, peeled and crushed; $1/2$ tsp minced chilli; 2 tbsp chopped coriander and 1 tbsp soy sauce. Prepare dumplings as above.

Cook's note: If not cooking immediately, place prepared dumplings on a plate sprinkled with a little cornflour to prevent sticking, loosely cover and chill until ready to cook. Prepared wontons can also be frozen for a week or two.

steamed prawn dumplings at top, eggplants at markets below

tua tua fritters

- Prepare: 5 minutes, plus standing
- Cook: 12 minutes (per batch) • Serves 4

Any kind of shellfish can be used for these
tasty, tender fritters. The mixture can be made
ahead of time and chilled for a few hours
before cooking – pack it into a chilled container
for a beachside barbecue. The fritters cook
well on a barbecue hot-plate or in a frypan.
Serve with a Jungle Herb Salad✿.

1.6kg (3^1/$_2$lb) fresh, live shellfish, eg. tua tuas
or pipis, washed, or 1 cup pre-cooked shellfish
flesh (if using, ignore first step)

2 tbsp water

pinch garam masala

^{1}/$_4$ cup self-raising flour

1 egg

2 tbsp milk

salt and freshly ground black pepper

oil or butter for barbecuing

PLACE shellfish in a large pot with 2 tbsp water.
Cover tightly and cook only for as long as it
takes for the shells to open (discard any that
don't). Remove flesh from shells.

PLACE flesh in a food processor and purée until
semi-smooth. Mix in all other ingredients (except
oil or butter for barbecuing) and blend until
evenly combined. Stand mixture for 10 minutes.

HEAT a barbecue hot-plate or frypan with a little
oil or butter and fry spoonfuls of the mixture
over medium heat. Turn as bubbles form on the
surface to cook other side.

Cook's note: If shellfish are sandy, place in a
bucket of cold seawater, sprinkle with flour or
rolled oats and leave in a cool place for
8-12 hours (they will spit out their sand).

soy and ginger salmon skewers

- Prepare: 10 minutes, plus standing
- Cook: 2-3 minutes • Makes 20-25 skewers

Thin slivers of fresh salmon are soaked in a teriyaki-style sauce before quickly grilling. Serve warm or at room temperature, as finger food or for a barbecue. The marinade is superb with all kinds of fish.

> 600-700g (1^1/$_2$lb) fresh, boneless and skinless salmon
>
> 2 tbsp soy sauce or tamari
>
> 1 tbsp sake (see pg 81)
>
> 1 tsp minced fresh ginger
>
> 1 tsp brown sugar
>
> 1 tsp sesame oil

SLICE salmon thinly on a slight angle across the fillet in 1cm (^{1}/$_2$in) slices. Mix soy sauce or tamari, sake, ginger, sugar and sesame oil through fish to evenly combine. Stand for 5-10 minutes (or up to 2 hours in the fridge).

HEAT grill. Thread slices of salmon onto bamboo skewers in a concertina fashion. Cover ends of skewers with foil to prevent them burning. Arrange skewers in a shallow baking tray. Place under a hot grill for 2-3 minutes until salmon has 'set' and is starting to caramelise on top. (Alternatively, cook quickly on a hot barbecue.)

Cook's note: Tamari is a rich, dark, Japanese soy sauce brewed without wheat – a remnant of the soy-sauce methods used in ancient China.

duck wontons

- Prepare: 10 minutes • Cook: 15 minutes
- Makes 20

Mini muffin tins make perfect moulds for crisp wonton cases. Here I have used a homemade Tamarind Dipping Sauce♥ to moisten the duck, but oyster, hoisin or the Chinese plum sauce that often comes in the packet with cooked Chinese roast duck also works well.

> 20 wonton wrappers
>
> oil spray or flavourless oil (eg. grapeseed) to brush wrappers
>
> 2 cups finely shredded roast duck (see pg 132) or chicken
>
> 3 tbsp Tamarind Dipping Sauce♥
>
> 2 tbsp finely chopped coriander

HEAT oven to 180°C (350°F/gas 4). Press wonton wrappers into mini muffin tins. Spray or brush with oil to lightly coat. Bake for 15 minutes until pale gold and crisp. Remove from oven and cool.

MIX shredded duck or chicken with Tamarind Dipping Sauce and coriander. Use mixture to fill wonton cases.

Cook's notes:
- Wonton wrappers are available frozen in the supermarket or fresh from Asian food stores (always check the 'use by' date). Thaw before using. They dry out easily once opened and become brittle around the edges. Wrap leftover wrappers in a damp paper towel and then seal in plastic wrap. They will keep for a few days in the fridge, or can be frozen.
- Baked wonton cases (without the filling) will keep in a sealed container for at least a week.

DRINKING KAVA
AT THE NAKAMAL

Advertised by a small lantern
outside the door, the Nakamal
is nothing more than a rough
bamboo shack. Inside, all is dark,
but for a thin thread of light
at the far end of the room,
where I can just make out the
figure of a man who is scooping
half-coconut shells of kava from
a large communal bowl.
Muted conversations emerge from
the shadows, broken by a barrage
of hoicking and spitting (it's a
good place to wear shoes).
Once an exclusive male-only
domain, Nakamal is now the common
name given to drinking houses
frequented by both sexes. Each bar
sells its own strength and flavour
of kava; a shell will set you back
less than 100 vatu (10c). The brown
dishwater liquid is thrown back
in one gulp. Muddy and slightly
peppery it has a numbing effect
in the mouth. After 4 cups my mind
feels clear and calm but my stomach
is churning. It's time for bed.

Luganville, September 1999.

spicy chicken cakes

• Prepare: 10 minutes • Cook: 4-6 minutes
(per batch) • Makes about 30 small patties

Fresh chicken and aromatic flavours are quickly
puréed then pan-fried for these easy, delicious
patties. Wonderful with Tropical Fruit Chutney✿,
Chilli Sauce✿ or Spicy Peanut Sauce✿.

300g (11oz) lean skinless chicken,
roughly chopped

small handful coriander leaves

1 spring onion, finely sliced

finely grated rind 1 lime or lemon (no pith)

2 tbsp Thai sweet chilli sauce

1 egg white

salt and freshly ground black pepper

$^1/_4$ cup coconut cream

flavourless oil (eg. grapeseed) for frying

PLACE all ingredients, except coconut cream
and oil, in a food processor and blend to a
coarse purée. Add coconut cream in a slow
stream until evenly absorbed.

HEAT a lightly oiled frypan. Drop heaped
teaspoonfuls of the mixture into the pan and
cook for about 2-3 minutes on each side over
medium heat.

Cook's notes:
• The patties can be made ahead of time and
quickly reheated in a hot oven.
• Fried vermicelli makes an attractive garnish for
finger foods as well as salads: put whole shank
of noodles into a big bag. Break noodles apart
thoroughly – they are quite tough and you'll
make a huge mess if you try to do this on the
bench. Heat oil and deep-fry noodles in handfuls.
They will puff up into a 'nest' in a few seconds.
Remove with a slotted spoon and drain on paper
towels. Store in an airtight container and they will
keep for weeks. If noodles soften, re-crisp in a
180°C (350°F/gas 4) oven for 5-6 minutes.

tuna patties with wasabi and soy

• Prepare: 5 minutes • Cook: 3 minutes
• Makes 10-12 small patties or 4 hamburger-
sized patties

This is a great combination. The very freshest
tuna (or salmon) is needed. The belly flesh –
toro tuna – is best. The mixture is also delicious
made into 4 large patties and lightly cooked for
hamburgers or hot sandwiches. Patties can be
prepared ahead of time and quickly reheated.
Serve with Fresh Mango Salsa (see below).

300g (11oz) piece freshest boneless tuna
or salmon

2 tsp wasabi powder (or 1 tsp paste)

2 tsp light soy sauce

finely grated rind 1 lime or lemon (no pith)

sesame oil for frying

CUT tuna or salmon into very fine dice. Mix the
wasabi with the soy and lime or lemon rind and
stir into the fish. Shape mixture into 10-12 patties.

HEAT a little oil in a large frypan and shallow-fry
patties for $1^1/_2$ minutes. Flip over and cook for
another minute.

fresh mango salsa

• Prepare: 3 minutes • Makes 2 cups

2 mangos (or 1 x 425g/15oz can, drained),
peeled and flesh chopped

2 tbsp Thai sweet chilli sauce

2 tbsp fresh lime or lemon juice

2 tbsp chopped fresh coriander

COMBINE all ingredients. Chill in the fridge until
ready to serve. Salsa will keep for up to 12 hours.

spicy chicken cakes on edible banana flower with a
garnish of fried vermicelli at top; tuna patties with
wasabi and soy, topped with fresh mango salsa below

coconut kaffir rice balls

- Prepare: 2 minutes, plus standing
- Cook: 30 minutes • Makes 24 rice balls

These flavoursome rice morsels combine traditional sushi rice with the fragrant flavour of kaffir lime, raw salmon and coconut for an appealing appetiser.

1 cup short-grain rice

3 tbsp lime or lemon juice

1 tsp sugar

$1/2$ tsp salt

$1/4$ cup desiccated coconut (see pg 146)

$1^1/4$ cups water

2 double kaffir lime leaves, central stem removed and leaves finely shredded

2 tbsp finely chopped pickled ginger

100g (4oz) fresh, raw salmon, very finely chopped

$1/4$ cup toasted black and white sesame seeds

WASH rice. Stand in cold water for 30 minutes. Drain thoroughly.

HEAT lime or lemon juice, sugar and salt in a small pot, stirring until dissolved. Put to one side.

PLACE drained rice in a pot with coconut and water. Bring to a boil over high heat. As soon as rice comes to the boil, reduce heat to lowest setting. Cover pot and cook for 12 minutes.

REMOVE from heat and stand for 15 minutes without uncovering. Mix through lime-juice mixture and kaffir lime leaves. Allow to cool (the rice can be chilled for up to 48 hours, covered in plastic wrap to prevent drying).

MIX through ginger and salmon to combine. Use wet hands to roll mixture into small balls. Roll balls in toasted sesame seeds.

Cook's note: Mild and tender new-season ginger is used to make pickled ginger. It is delicious with raw fish, sushi and salads. Buy it at Asian or Japanese food stores.

pacific tuna tartare

- Prepare: 10 minutes • Makes enough for 10 small open sandwiches

Use the very freshest tuna for this simple finger food.

100g (4oz) fresh, boneless tuna or salmon, very finely chopped

1 tbsp chopped fresh mint leaves

1 double kaffir lime leaf, central stem removed, leaf finely shredded

$1/4$ tsp minced fresh red chilli

1 tbsp extra-virgin olive oil, plus extra to drizzle

$1/2$ tsp finely grated lime or lemon rind (no pith), plus 10 very thin slices lime or lemon to garnish

10 thin slices rustic bread (eg. ciabatta)

salt and freshly ground black pepper

COMBINE tuna or salmon with the mint, shredded kaffir lime leaf, chilli, olive oil and lime or lemon rind.

SPOON mixture onto bread and season with salt and pepper. Top with a slice of lime or lemon and drizzle with a splash of olive oil. Serve at once.

Cook's note: The ingredients can be combined and left to chill in the fridge a few hours before spooning onto bread.

pacific tuna tartare at top, double kaffir lime leaves below

KAFFIR LIMES

(citrus hystrix)

Kaffir lime trees flourish in
frost-free climates and grow well
in a pot on the deck. They take
years to fruit but, in fact, while the
rind of the fruit is delicious, it is the
leaves which provide the cook
with an exquisitely fragrant
citrus flavouring.

Kaffir - the allure of citrus

Fresh kaffir lime leaves can be
found in Asian food stores; they
also freeze well. Add whole leaves
to liquids to infuse, or remove the
tough central stem, shred finely and
add to salads, stir-fries and curries.
The leaves impart a bitter flavour
if used in excess. Whole fresh
kaffir limes can be frozen –
the rinds remove easily before
the fruit has thawed.

rum and pineapple cocktail

• Prepare: 5 minutes • Makes 1 large drink

$\frac{1}{3}$ glass Jamaican rum (eg, Appletons rum)

1 capful Malibu

4-5 ice cubes

chilled pineapple juice to fill glass

POUR rum and Malibu over ice cubes in a tall glass. Top with chilled pineapple juice. Stir and serve straightaway.

kiwi-coladas

• Prepare: 5 minutes • Makes 5-6 cocktails

2 cups frozen kiwifruit juice, thawed, or 500ml (1 pint) kiwifruit purée, chilled

1 cup chilled coconut cream

1 – 2 tsp honey

1 cup white rum

3 tbsp Cointreau

2 cups ice cubes

BLEND all ingredients together. Serve straightaway.

mango sunrise

• Prepare: 5 minutes • Makes 4 cocktails

1 x 425g (15oz) can mango slices in natural juice

$\frac{1}{2}$ cup chilled vodka

3 tbsp fresh lime juice

2-3 tsp icing sugar

2 cups ice cubes

BLEND all ingredients until smooth and sludgy. Serve straightaway.

passionfruit and pineapple daiquiris

• Prepare: 5 minutes • Makes 4 cocktails

1 large banana, peeled

$\frac{1}{4}$ cup Preserved Passionfruit Syrup✿ or sieved pulp 2 fresh passionfruit

2 cups pineapple juice

$\frac{1}{2}$ cup white rum

3 tbsp Cointreau

dash Angostura Bitters

2 cups ice cubes

PLACE everything in a blender and purée until smooth. Serve straightaway.

jade slippers

• Prepare: 5 minutes • Makes 1 large drink

2 capfuls gin

1 capful Midori

4-5 ice cubes

1 tbsp fresh lime juice

chilled soda or lemonade to fill glass

POUR gin and Midori over ice cubes in a tall glass. Add lime juice and top with soda or lemonade.

rum and pineapple cocktails

salmon and sweet-potato cakes

• Prepare: 10 minutes • Cook: 6-8 minutes
(per batch) • Makes 12 patties

These delicate patties combine grated
par-cooked sweet potato with fresh salmon.
Chop the fish finely, otherwise the patties
tend to fall apart on cooking.

1 medium-sized kumara or other sweet potato
(about 175g/6oz)

250g (9oz) fresh salmon, finely chopped into
1cm ($^1/_3$in) pieces

1 egg white, lightly beaten

grated rind $^1/_2$ lime or lemon (no pith)

1 tbsp finely sliced spring onion

salt and freshly ground black pepper

about 2 tbsp rice flour or plain flour to
lightly coat

3-4 tbsp oil

PEEL and cut kumara or sweet potato into
large chunks and boil in salted water for
5 minutes. Meanwhile, combine salmon with
egg white, lime or lemon rind, spring onion
and salt and pepper.

DRAIN and cool kumara, then grate coarsely
and mix into the salmon. Form mixture into
large walnut-sized balls, roll in flour to lightly
coat. Flatten to form patties.

HEAT oil in a heavy frypan and fry patties,
in batches, over medium heat for 3-4 minutes
until golden and crusty on the base, then turn
carefully to cook and brown other side. Place
cooked patties on paper towels to remove
excess oil.

Cook's note: These little savoury patties re-heat
well. Place on a baking tray in a 180°C (350°F/
gas 4) oven for 5 minutes.

BANANA POKE

The national dish of Rarotonga,
and one which you will find in the
markets, banana poke is made by
mashing bananas to a pulp, then
cooking very slowly for up to two
hours in a heavy pot. For every two
cups of cooked pulp, one cup
arrowroot starch is added, plus a little
sugar, if needed. The mixture is baked
in a shallow dish for about an hour
until browned, then served in scoops
with fresh coconut cream.

salmon and sweet potato cakes at top,
vegetable pakoras below

vegetable pakoras

- Prepare: 5 minutes, plus standing
- Cook: 3-5 minutes (per batch) • Makes about 12

A batter made with chickpea flour and water and flavoured with spices is mixed with chopped vegetables and quickly fried for a tasty finger food. Serve with Tamarind Dipping Sauce♡ or Cucumber and Banana Raita♡.

$^3/_4$ cup chickpea flour or Besan

$^1/_2$ tsp ground cumin

$^1/_2$ tsp mustard seeds

1 tsp curry powder

1 clove garlic, peeled and crushed

$^1/_2$ cup cold water

1 cup chopped mixed vegetables (eg. $^1/_3$ cup grated carrot, $^1/_3$ cup blanched and chopped broccoli, $^1/_3$ cup peas or chopped sugar snaps)

2 tbsp fresh coriander

salt and freshly ground black pepper

$^1/_4$ tsp baking soda, crushed to remove lumps

flavourless oil (eg. grapeseed) for frying

COMBINE chickpea flour with spices, garlic and water to form a smooth batter. Mix in vegetables, coriander, salt and pepper and baking soda. Stand for 5-10 minutes.

HEAT 3-4cm (1$^1/_2$in) oil in a deep frypan and deep-fry small spoonfuls of pakora mixture – in batches of 3-4 at a time – for about 3 minutes until golden and cooked through. Remove from oil, shake off excess and place on paper towels.

Cook's notes:
- Chickpea flour is pale yellow and has a high protein content. It is commonly used in Indian cooking for batters and fritters. Ask for it by the name of Besan in Asian food stores.
- When deep-frying the pakoras, don't have the oil too hot or they will burn before they have fully cooked in the middle.
- Cooked pakoras can be reheated in a hot oven for a few minutes.

THE TRADITIONAL PACIFIC DIET

The traditional Pacific diet revolves around the tropical starches – yams, taro, sweet potato, banana, breadfruit, cassava (tapioca), sago and Polynesian arrowroot. Wild vegetables, roots, fruits and nuts are harvested, and gardens cultivated for root crops and fruit. Collecting seafood and catching fish is an important daily ritual. Coconut cream is the central thread throughout. Anointing everything both raw and cooked, it provides a vehicle for flavour and is a rich source of the fat that makes skins glow like burnished mahogany. Although a diverse range of spices and herbs grows freely, they tend not to be included in island food preparation. Tradition deems that nothing more than coconut cream be added. The result – at least to the Western palate – tastes extraordinarily bland.

sweet-potato crisps

• Prepare: 10 minutes • Cook: 5 minutes (per batch) • Makes 24-30 large chips

Golden kumara makes the crispest chips. However, all types of sweet potato work well, as do cassava, taro and plantain.

3 sweet potatoes, preferably more rectangular than round

flavourless oil (eg. grapeseed) for frying

PEEL sweet potatoes. Slice lengthwise very thinly using a Benriner, mandolin or large vegetable peeler.

HEAT 4cm (1$\frac{1}{2}$in) oil in a large heavy pot or deep frypan. Fry sweet-potato slices in batches over medium-high heat until crisp and golden – about 5 minutes. Shake off excess oil over pan and drain on paper towels.

Variations:
• To make cassava crisps, boil peeled cassava tubers in lightly salted water until tender. (If cassava is frozen, do not thaw before cooking.) Drain thoroughly and allow to cool. Cut in half and remove woody core. Slice thinly into chips. Deep-fry in hot oil until pale gold and crisp. Dry on paper towels.
• To make taro crisps, boil peeled taro tubers in lightly salted water for 45 minutes or until tender. Drain thoroughly and prepare as main recipe.
• To make plantain chips, boil 2 whole green plantain with their skins on for 15 minutes. Cool, peel and angle-slice into pieces about 1.5cm ($\frac{1}{2}$in) thick. Shallow-fry for 2-3 minutes each side until golden and crisp.

Cook's notes:
• Take care not to have the oil too hot – a cube of bread should turn pale gold in about 40 seconds.
• Crisps will keep fresh in an airtight container for over a week. If they soften, they can be re-crisped in a hot oven for a few minutes.
• A Benriner is a useful food slicer available from Asian foodstores.

The isolation of the Pacific, the sheer vastness of water with scattered constellations of tiny islands, made for a solitary existence. To the ancient seafarers of the Pacific, the universe comprised the ocean as far as they could traverse it, the heavens above with their guiding stars, their gods and the underworld of spirits. Sacrifices to ensure good harvests and safe passages were part of everyday life, and omens read in the waters and the sky.

Even today, many tribes live by their legends, maintaining traditional rituals in the production, harvesting and storage of food. Tapu, the forbidding law, was used – and is still today – to protect resources and safeguard traditions that maintain the integrity of the culture. In some islands, women are forbidden from handling certain crops, such as yams, as it is believed they will pollute and 'devalue' the harvest.

feasts around a fire

There are pigs to kill, chickens to pluck, dances and songs and drumbeats to waken the night. A feast…

In 1846, in a feast held to celebrate peace between two New Zealand tribes, revellers gorged on 50,000 eels, 900 pigs and 8000 baskets of kumara and potatoes. All cooked in hangi ovens under the earth.

To prepare a hangi, a pit about knee-deep is dug and lined with leaves. In it, a fire is built to heat fist-sized volcanic rocks.

After about an hour – the fire reduced to embers and the rocks hot enough to steam when splashed – the hangi is ready for cooking.

Onto a layer of wet sacks or leaves go baskets of food, layered with the slowest cooking items at the bottom. The food is covered with more leaves or sacks then a thick layer of soil shovelled over to cover the top. After 2-3 hours, the hangi is done – the flavours sweetly melded, smoky and rich.

roast lamb cutlets with chilli mint salsa

- Prepare: 10 minutes, plus marinating
- Cook: 8-10 minutes • Serves 6-8

Both the meat and the salsa can be prepared ahead of time (but add the mint and spring onions to the salsa just before serving to prevent browning). Cut the lamb racks into sections of 2-3 ribs per serve. Serve with a Sweet Potato Mash✿ and Wilted Watercress✿.

Chilli Mint Salsa: 2 tbsp sugar; 2 tbsp flavourless oil (eg. grapeseed); $1/4$ cup rice vinegar; juice and finely grated rind 1 lime (no pith); 1 tbsp fish sauce; 3 minced red chillies; 2 spring onions, finely sliced; 40 mint leaves

2 trimmed racks lamb, 10-12 bones each

2 tbsp fish sauce

2 cloves garlic, peeled and crushed

2 tbsp Thai sweet chilli sauce

2 tbsp chopped mint leaves

1 tbsp oil

salt and freshly ground black pepper

COMBINE all salsa ingredients except spring onions and mint leaves. Chill in fridge until serving (up to 24 hours). At serving time, pour boiling water over mint leaves, drain at once and chill under cold water. Drain and chop. Mix into salsa with spring onions.

CUT lamb racks into 2-3 rib cutlets. Combine fish sauce, garlic, chilli sauce and mint and mix through lamb. Chill for at least 30 minutes.

HEAT a frypan with oil. Season cutlets; brown over high heat for a minute each side. (The meat can be chilled until ready to finish cooking.)

HEAT oven to 220°C (425°F/gas 7).Transfer lamb to a roasting dish and cook for 6-8 minutes until done to your liking. Stand for 5 minutes before serving with the salsa.

COOKING A WHOLE PIG

Various sizes and types of animal can be cooked over a spit, but, in all cases, the meat needs frequent basting and a low, slow heat to ensure a moist, tender result. About two hours before cooking, prepare a large fire and rub Ginger Honey Glaze (see pg 128) over the whole pig and in the cavity.

Have a small bucket of water ready in case you need to douse flames caused by dripping fat. Have the spit 30-50cm (12-20in) above the glowing embers – it's the right height if you can hold your hand above the heat source for three seconds before it gets too hot.

Lift the pig from marinade and place on the spit. Cook, checking every 15 minutes or so for any flare-ups. After 2 hours, start brushing the pig with the marinade.

After $3^{1}/_{2}$-4 hours, the skin should be crispy, sticky and caramelised and the flesh cooked through. Simmer remaining marinade for 5 minutes and serve with the pig.

roast lamb cutlets with chilli mint salsa served on sweet potato mash with wilted watercress

chilli lime chicken and noodles

- Prepare: 10 minutes, plus marinating
- Cook: 5 minutes • Serves 4

The flavourings used here provide this simple noodle meal with a fresh, fragrant appeal. The marinade is also superb for barbecued chicken.

Chilli Lime Marinade: 1 tbsp minced fresh ginger; 1 clove garlic, peeled and crushed; 4 double kaffir lime leaves, finely shredded; 1 tsp grated palm sugar (see pg 143) or brown sugar; 1-2 red chillies, deseeded, pith removed and minced; finely grated rind 1 lime or lemon (no pith); 2 tbsp flavourless oil (eg, grapeseed)

500g (1lb) boneless, skinless chicken, chopped in 2cm (1in) pieces

750g (1$^{1}/_{2}$lb) fresh rice noodles or 250g (9oz) dry, soaked according to packet directions

2 handfuls snowpeas, angle sliced

2 spring onions, very finely sliced

$^{1}/_{4}$ cup fish sauce

$^{1}/_{4}$ cup Thai sweet chilli sauce

$^{1}/_{2}$ cup chopped mint or coriander

juice 1 lime or lemon

COMBINE marinade ingredients. Mix through chicken. Marinate in fridge for 15-30 minutes.

HEAT a heavy frypan and fry chicken until just cooked through. Microwave soaked noodles for 2 minutes, or drop into boiling water and drain immediately. Add to chicken with snowpeas and spring onions, stir over heat for a minute. Stir in fish sauce, chilli sauce and mint or coriander. Toss until heated through.

PILE onto serving plates and squeeze over lime or lemon juice.

WINTER DINNER

- papaya, avocado and prawn salad with curry mayo

- roast lamb cutlets with chilli mint salsa, sweet potato mash and wilted watercress

- grilled pineapple with rum and star anise

seared sesame salmon with udon noodles

• Prepare: 15 minutes • Cook: 4-5 minutes
• Serves 4 as a main or 6-8 as a first course

Here's a great dish for hassle-free entertaining. The fish is prepared in advance, needing only a quick flash in the oven before serving.

400-500g (1lb) fillet salmon, skin and bones removed

1 egg white, beaten until fluffy

1 tbsp each white and black sesame seeds

2 tbsp oil

500g (1lb) packet fresh udon noodles or cooked spaghetti

Japanese Dressing: 4 tbsp rice wine or white wine vinegar; 3 tbsp flavourless oil (eg. grapeseed); $1^{1}/_{2}$ tbsp soy sauce; 2 tsp sesame oil

$^{1}/_{2}$ cup shredded nori

2 spring onions, finely sliced

CUT salmon into 4 pieces. Brush tops with egg white. Press egg-white-coated side of salmon into sesame seeds to fully cover top.

HEAT oil in a large frypan and brown salmon – seed side only – over high heat, for about 30 seconds. Place, seed side up, in a single layer on a tray and chill in fridge until ready to serve.

HEAT oven to 200°C (400°F/gas 6) and grease or line a baking tray. Slice each piece of cold salmon into 3-4 equal slices. Lay slices, slightly overlapping, on the tray. Bake 3-4 minutes.

DROP udon noodles or spaghetti into boiling water for a few seconds to heat through.

COMBINE dressing ingredients. Mix noodles with shredded nori, spring onions and three-quarters of dressing. Divide among 4 bowls. Carefully lift salmon slices off tray and arrange on noodles. Spoon over remaining dressing.

BAMBOO TO COOK AND PRESERVE

Up until 60 years ago, much of the food in the islands of Vanuatu was cooked in bamboo tubes (including human flesh!). Today, restaurants serve green bamboo stuffed with various combinations of vegetables, chicken seafood and rice. Bamboo is also used in this tropical climate to preserve meat for short periods – hunters on three- or four-day forays chop and pack their kill into tubes of fresh bamboo, seal it with a plug of leaves and then throw it into the fire for 30-40 minutes. Now it will keep for up to a week.

ginger sake roast beef

- Prepare: 5 minutes • Cook: 30-35 minutes
- Serves 4

Here's a quick, flavoursome treatment for a fillet of beef. While the meat 'rests', a light sauce is made in the pan. As fillet is a lean cut, take care not to overcook it. I like to serve it with Taro Crisps✿ or Cassava Crisps✿ and Lightly Cooked Asian Greens✿.

2 cloves garlic, peeled and crushed

3 tsp minced fresh ginger

2 tbsp grated palm sugar (see pg 143) or brown sugar

600g-800g (1½lb) piece beef fillet from thick end

salt and freshly ground black pepper

oil for searing

1 tbsp oyster sauce (see pg 130)

1 tsp tomato paste

¼ cup sake (see pg 81)

1 cup water or beef stock

finely grated rind ½ orange (no pith)

HEAT oven to 220°C (425°F/gas 7). Rub garlic, 2 tsp ginger and all sugar into beef. Season with salt and lots of black pepper.

HEAT a heavy frying pan with a little oil over high heat and sear meat all over to lightly brown. Transfer to a shallow roasting dish. Spread oyster sauce over meat.

ROAST beef for 20-25 minutes, turning after 10 minutes, until meat feels slightly springy. Rest in a warm place for 10 minutes.

PLACE tomato paste in the browning pan (don't wash it, as the meat juices add to the flavour of the sauce) and stir over heat for 1 minute. Mix in remaining tsp of ginger, the sake, water or stock and orange rind, stirring to lift flavours from the pan. Bring to a fast boil. Serve spooned over or around meat.

kava leaves at top, ginger sake roast beef served with cassava and taro crisps and asian greens below

satay pork skewers

- Prepare: 10 minutes, plus marinating
- Cook: 4-6 minutes • Makes 18-20 (serves 6)

The marinade used here is wonderful with pork or chicken, and it can also be boiled and served as a sauce. As an alternative, the recipe for Asian Barbecue Sauce✿ also works well as a marinade. I like to serve the skewers on a bed of Green Papaya and Vermicelli Salad✿, but they are also good with baked kumara or Chinese Slaw✿.

Satay Marinade: 3 cloves garlic, peeled and chopped; 3cm (1in) piece ginger, peeled and grated; 2 tbsp soy sauce; 3 tbsp Thai sweet chilli sauce; 1 tbsp fish sauce; 2 tbsp peanut butter; $^1/_2$ cup coconut cream; 2 spring onions, finely sliced; handful coriander leaves, chopped

2 pork fillets, each halved crosswise, then each half cut lengthwise into thin $^1/_2$ cm ($^1/_3$ in) strips

COMBINE marinade ingredients. Mix through pork. Cover and chill in the fridge for at least an hour (up to 24). Meanwhile, soak 18-20 wooden barbecue skewers in cold water and heat grill.

LIFT meat from marinade. Thread strips of meat lengthwise onto skewers, concertina style. Cover ends of skewers with foil to prevent them burning. Grill – close to heat source – for 2-3 minutes on each side until starting to brown.

BOIL marinade for 5 minutes while meat cooks. Dunk cooked skewers (without the foil) into boiled marinade to glaze and serve extra sauce in a jug on the side.

Cook's note: Vermicelli, known also as bean-thread or cellophane noodles, is often found in the produce department at the supermarket. The clear, brittle strands soften after soaking in hot water for a few minutes. Packets containing individually wrapped small bundles are the most useful, as the large packets contain one vast hank which makes a real mess when you separate it. For easiest handling, put the whole packet into a paper bag and use scissors to separate them.

satay pork skewers served on green papaya and vermicelli salad at top, cultivated taro below

jungle chicken curry

- Prepare: 15 minutes • Cook: 15 minutes
- Serves 6

The base for this curry can be used for beef, pork, fish or seafood. Don't be put off by the long list of ingredients – it's dead easy and the flavour is delicious. Accompany with Coconut Rice❂ and Fresh Banana Salad❂.

Jungle Flavour Paste: 2 tbsp oil, 2 tbsp crushed garlic, 2 tbsp minced fresh ginger, 1 tsp shrimp paste, 1 tbsp minced red chilli, 1 tbsp minced lemongrass, 1 tbsp curry powder, 2 tsp grated palm sugar (see pg 143) or brown sugar

2 tbsp peanut butter

2 cups coconut milk

2 cups chicken stock

1 tbsp fish sauce

3 sweet potatoes, peeled and chopped into 3cm (1in) cubes

600g (1¼lb) boneless, skinless chicken, thinly sliced

Garnish: selection of beansprouts; watercress and fresh coriander, chopped; spring onions, finely chopped; chilli, deseeded, pith removed and finely sliced; basil or Vietnamese mint leaves, chopped

MAKE paste by heating oil in a heavy pot, add remaining paste ingredients and gently fry.

MIX peanut butter with a little of the coconut milk to thin, add to paste in pot with rest of coconut milk, stock and fish sauce. Bring to a simmer.

ADD sweet potato to sauce, simmer 10 minutes then add chicken and simmer 4-5 minutes until cooked through. Serve in bowls topped with your selection of garnish ingredients.

Variation: Peeled and chopped pumpkin, potatoes or taro can be used in place of sweet potato.

Cook's note: The sauce, without the chicken and sweet potato, will keep in the fridge for up to 2 days.

spicy beef salad

- Prepare: 10 minutes • Cook: 4-6 minutes
- Serves 2

Variations on this theme abound. I particularly like the fresh zing of crunchy vegetables, tender beef and tangy chilli dressing in this simple version.

1 tbsp oil for frying

salt and freshly ground black pepper

1 x 200-220g (7-8oz) thick-cut, premium-quality beef steak (sirloin, rump or fillet), fat and sinew removed

Sweet Chilli Dressing: 3 tbsp Thai sweet chilli sauce, 1 tbsp fish sauce, 1 tsp brown sugar, ¼ cup fresh lime or lemon juice

½ telegraph cucumber, chopped into small finger-sized batons

½ red onion, peeled and chopped into very thin wedges

6-8 cherry tomatoes, halved

2 spring onions, finely sliced

handful sugar snap peas, finely sliced (optional)

¼ cup each chopped mint and coriander

soft lettuce leaves

HEAT oil in a large frypan. Season beef and cook 2-3 minutes each side until medium rare. Set aside to cool and, meanwhile, combine dressing ingredients.

PLACE cucumber, onion, tomatoes, spring onions and sugar snap peas in a bowl with the herbs. Drizzle over half the dressing and toss to coat thoroughly. Thinly slice the cooked meat across the grain and toss through the salad.

TO SERVE, arrange a bed of lettuce leaves on a serving plate. Pile salad on top and drizzle over remaining dressing.

FIRE WITHOUT MATCHES

Vincent and his brothers are
playing the tamtam, sing-songing
the stories of the old days in high
crooning tones. The tales of these
old men – WWll vets now well into
their eighties – trace their family
lineage here back 600 years.

The white-haired Vincent
whittles a piece of namatal wood,
then rubs it in short fast strokes
across a larger piece of wood.
Soon a small pile of fine sawdust
has accumulated at the far end and,
presto, there is fire. "No matches,
huh?" He takes the cigarette from
behind his ear and lights it.
"Never go hungry here." He laughs,
revealing, for all his years,
a mouthful of beautiful strong
white teeth.

Bethlehem Village, September 1999

kashmiri lamb skewers

• Prepare: 10 minutes, plus marinating
• Cook: 5 minutes (per batch), plus 2-3 minutes
on the barbecue • Makes 18 skewers

These fabulous little skewers are par-boiled
ahead of time to prevent them from falling apart
on the grill and over-charring. They're delicious
accompanied with Cucumber and Banana Raita✿.
I like to use wooden chopsticks to skewer the
mixture – you'll find bulk packs of disposables
(you'll need 18-20) at Asian food stores.

    1 tsp cumin seeds

    1 tsp cardamom seeds

    1 tbsp flavourless oil (eg, grapeseed)

    1 tsp curry powder

    2 cloves garlic, peeled and crushed

    1 tsp minced fresh ginger

    500g (1lb) coarsely minced lean lamb

    1 tsp brown sugar

    juice 1 lime or $^1/_2$ lemon

    salt and freshly ground black pepper

    $^1/_4$ cup chopped coriander

GRIND cumin and cardamom with a mortar and
pestle. Heat oil in a small frypan and fry ground
spices with curry powder, garlic and ginger
for about a minute until fragrant. Remove from
heat and add to lamb, along with sugar, lime
or lemon juice, salt and pepper and coriander.
Combine and place in fridge for at least an
hour to marinate.

BRING a large pot of water to the boil. Mould
a small handful of the mixture around each
chopstick. Drop 3-4 skewers at a time into
boiling water and cook for about 5 minutes
until meat is just 'set'. Chill until ready to serve.

WRAP ends of chopsticks in foil to prevent
charring. Pop sticks onto a heated barbecue
plate and cook for 2-3 minutes until browned.

slow-braised pork with udon noodles

• Prepare: 20 minutes • Cook: 2$^3/_4$ hours
• Serves 6

This succulent pork dish can be cooked a
day or two ahead of time. I like to quickly
roast the cooked meat in a very hot oven just
before serving to get it crispy.

    1.3-1.5kg (3lb) meaty pork pieces (cut from belly)

    2 litres (3$^1/_2$ pints) hot water

    $^3/_4$ cup sake (see pg 81) or sherry

    1 cup light soy sauce

    1 tbsp liquid honey

    4 whole star anise (see pg 151)

    1 whole cinnamon stick

    30 very thin slices fresh ginger

    1-2 whole red chillies (fresh or dried)

    1 whole head garlic, cloves peeled and halved

    1 tbsp rice vinegar or cider vinegar

    400g (14oz) udon noodles

    2 spring onions, cut in long thin strips

    2 tsp sesame oil

PLACE pork in a pot (it should fit snugly in a
single layer). Add hot water and bring to a
simmer, removing scum as it appears. After
30 minutes, add other ingredients – except
noodles, spring onions and sesame oil – cover
and simmer over a very low heat for 2 hours,
turning meat twice. (Alternatively, transfer to a
170°C/325°F/gas 3 oven and bake, covered, for
2$^1/_2$ hours.) The dish can be prepared to this
point and chilled for up to 48 hours.

HEAT oven to 220°C (425°F/gas 7). Lift meat out
of pot (reserving liquid) and place in a shallow
roasting dish. Roast in oven 10-15 minutes until it
crisps. Boil liquid for 10 minutes until syrupy.

POUR boiling water over noodles and stand
2 minutes. Drain and toss with spring onions and
sesame oil. Divide noodles between bowls, top
with meat and spoon over the cooking sauce.

kashmiri lamb skewers served with cucumber and banana
raita at top, slow braised pork with udon noodles below

roasted pork with ginger honey glaze

- Prepare: 15 minutes, plus marinating
- Cook: 60-80 minutes • Serves 8

The glaze used here is one of my favourites. It is also delicious with barbecued pork or a whole suckling pig. (You'll find information on cooking a whole baby pig on pg 119). Serve with Caramelised Pineapple and Kumara❀.

Ginger Honey Glaze: 2 tbsp finely chopped fresh ginger; 1 spring onion, finely sliced; 3 cloves garlic, peeled and finely chopped; $^1/_4$ cup honey; $^1/_2$ cup pineapple juice; 2 tbsp soy sauce; 1 tbsp toasted sesame oil; 2 star anise (see pg 151); 2 red chillies, deseeded, pith removed and minced

1 loin pork, about 1.4kg (3lb), skin cut off and reserved

2 cups pineapple juice

salt

PLACE glaze ingredients in a pot and bring to a boil. Cool. Cut deep slashes, diagonally, over the pork loin about 3cm ($1^1/_4$in) apart. Place pork in a bowl and pour over glaze. Cover and marinate overnight in the fridge.

HEAT oven to 200°C (400°F/gas 6). Transfer pork to a roasting dish (reserving glaze). Pour pineapple juice over pork and cook, covered, for 45 minutes. Uncover and brush meat with glaze. Cook further 15-25 minutes or until juices run clear when a skewer is inserted into the deepest part of the meat. Stand for 10 minutes before carving into thick slices.

PREPARE crackling while pork cooks. Cut pork skin into 8-10 pieces, score lightly on the skin side. Place in a dish, brush with water, sprinkle with salt and roast for about 20 minutes until crisp and golden. Drain off fat. Serve pieces on top of pork with pan juices poured over.

Cook's note: The glaze will keep in the fridge for a few weeks. Boil it each time after marinating raw meat.

lemongrass and chilli risotto

- Prepare: 10 minutes • Cook: 20 minutes
- Serves 6

This risotto makes a great stand-alone dish, but when I'm having guests, I like to serve it with Lime and Coriander Flash-roasted Fish❀.

$^1/_4$ cup olive oil

1 red pepper, deseeded, pith removed and finely chopped

2 cups Arborio or other Italian short-grain risotto rice

5 cups boiling chicken or fish stock

2 tbsp minced lemongrass

4 double kaffir lime leaves, or finely grated rind 2 limes (no pith)

1 small red chilli, deseeded, pith removed and minced

salt and freshly ground black pepper

$^1/_4$ cup lime or lemon juice, plus lime or lemon wedges to serve

3 tbsp chopped coriander

2-3 tbsp Thai sweet chilli sauce

HEAT oil in a heavy-bottomed pot and gently fry peppers for a couple of minutes. Add rice and stir for a couple of minutes over heat to coat the grains in oil. Add stock, lemongrass, kaffir lime leaves or rind, chilli and a little salt. Cover and simmer on lowest heat for 20 minutes, stirring frequently.

MIX in lime or lemon juice, coriander and chilli sauce. Cover and stand for 2-3 minutes to allow flavours to absorb. Adjust seasoning to taste. Serve with wedges of lime.

Cook's note: Leftover risotto can be spread onto a tray, chilled, then cut into wedges and grilled or fried.

lemongrass at top, lemongrass and chilli risotto with lime and coriander flash-roasted fish below

LEMONGRASS
(cymbopogon citratus)

Lemongrass can be grown in a temperate environment provided there is sufficient water. Discard the leaves, which are very sharp, and trim the stems to 8-10cm (3-4in) in length. Lemongrass loses flavour when dried, but will store in the fridge for about a week and can be frozen. Two to three strips of lemon peel can be used as a substitute.

Lemongrass – a fragrant balm

The straggly appearance of this almost woody tropical grass belies its subtle lemon perfume and balm-like flavour. Bruise the whole stem and add to stocks and broths to infuse a delicate citrus flavour, or peel back the outer leaves around the base to reveal the tender white core which can be sliced or pounded to a paste.

RITUALS OF THE YAM HARVEST

On the island of Pentecost, the annual Naghol, forerunner of the modern bungy jump, is undertaken each April or May. For centuries, this life-risking ceremony has been performed to ensure a successful yam crop.

As well as being a common food throughout the Pacific, yams are important in many rituals, and are used as trading currency, along with pigs, to buy wives and seal arrangements.

Without the aid of wires, saws or hammers, each 30m (100ft) tower for the Naghol takes about five weeks to construct using saplings, vines and materials from the surrounding jungle. On it, each 'land-diver' builds his own launch platform and must select his own vines to tie around his ankles and tether him to the tower. Too short and he risks breaking bones on the rebound; too long and his skull will be crushed on the ground.

glazed barbecue quail or chicken

- **Prepare: 10 minutes, plus marinating**
- **Cook: 10-12 minutes for quail, 12-14 minutes for chicken • Serves 4 as a main or 6-8 as part of a range of barbecue dishes**

If you've never cooked quail before, give it a go – it's easy and the taste is superb. If the butcher doesn't stock it, ask him to order it for you. It's not cheap, so you may just want to serve half a bird per person. Unlike chicken, which needs to be cooked thoroughly, quail is best served slightly rare. Here, I've served it with Sesame Grilled Vegetables✿.

4 quails, quartered (or 400g/14oz chicken breasts)

2 cloves garlic, peeled and crushed

1 tbsp minced fresh ginger

1 tsp minced red chilli

1 tsp brown sugar

2 tsp fish sauce

2 tbsp oyster sauce

MIX quail or chicken with garlic, ginger, chilli, brown sugar and fish sauce. Marinate in the fridge for at least 30 minutes (up to 24 hours).

HEAT a barbecue hot-plate and cook, allowing 10-12 minutes for quail and 12-14 minutes for chicken. Brush with oyster sauce towards the end of cooking to glaze.

Cook's notes:
- Oyster sauce has a smooth, silky texture, rich brown colour and a salty, slightly fishy flavour. Use 2-3 tablespoons to add flavour (aromatic but not fishy) to stir-fries, soups and dressings. Once opened, store in the fridge.
- Quail or chicken is also delicious marinated in Teriyaki Sauce✿.

glazed barbecue quail served with sesame grilled vegetables

duck and mango salad

- Prepare: 20 minutes
- Cook: 10 minutes (to crisp duck skin) • Serves 6

This is a great salad for a special occasion. All the components can be prepared in advance, ready for a quick, last-minute assembly.

1 roasted duck

25-30 snowpeas

3 ripe mangos, peeled and flesh chopped or 2 x 425g (15oz) cans mangos in juice, drained and chopped

2 spring onions, finely sliced

1 large red pepper, deseeded, pith removed and finely sliced

6 handfuls baby salad greens or spinach leaves

Dressing: $^{1}/_{2}$ cup orange juice, $^{1}/_{4}$ cup lime or lemon juice, 1 tsp grated palm sugar (see pg 143) or brown sugar, 1 tsp sesame oil, 1 free-range egg yolk (or 2 tbsp oil), salt and freshly ground black pepper

$^{1}/_{2}$ cup toasted cashew nuts

REMOVE skin from duck and place skin on a baking tray. Grill or roast until crispy. Drain off all fat and cut in thin strips. Put to one side.

SHRED duck meat, discarding fat and bones. Pour boiling water over snowpeas, cool at once under cold water, drain.

PLACE duck, skin, snowpeas in a large serving bowl with the mangos, spring onions, red pepper and salad greens or baby spinach leaves. Combine dressing ingredients; toss through salad. Garnish with cashew nuts.

Cook's note: Chinese grocers and takeout stores frequently sell hot roasted ducks. They are delicious, though can be quite fatty. Remove skin and meat while still warm. Roasted duck meat can be frozen. Use the carcass as the base for a noodle soup, flavoured with orange rind, ginger, chopped spring onions and a few whole star anise (see pg 151).

PALUSAMI

Young taro leaves and coconut cream are the principle ingredients of palusami, a universal dish of the South Pacific which is thoroughly delicious. To make this dish, a bed of taro leaves is layered in the palm of the hand, sometimes with cooked onion or a mixture of onion and either corned beef, chicken or fish. Coconut cream is poured on and the leaves folded over and wrapped to secure the contents. The taro parcel is then wrapped in more leaves or foil and baked for about an hour.

malaysian fish in rice-paper wraps

- Prepare: 15 minutes
- Cook: 3-4 minutes (per batch) • Makes 12 (serves 4-6)

These parcels look and taste stunning. They can be put together up to 8 hours ahead of time and chilled ready for a quick last-minute fry in the pan. Accompany with Lightly Cooked Asian Greens✪ and oyster or chilli sauce for a light main-course meal.

400g (14oz) fresh, boneless white fish, cut into 12 pieces 8cm x 4cm (3in x $1^1/_2$in)

1 spring onion, very finely chopped

1 tsp minced fresh ginger

1 tbsp fish sauce

2 tbsp Thai sweet chilli sauce

juice $^1/_2$ lemon

12 rounds rice paper

12 fresh coriander leaves or some chives for garnish

2 tbsp safflower or peanut oil to cook

PLACE fish pieces in a mixing bowl with all other ingredients except rice paper, coriander or chives, and oil. Mix to combine.

DIP a sheet of rice paper into very hot water, count to 2, remove and place on a damp clean cloth. The paper will soften in about 1 minute.

PLACE a piece of coated fish near the edge of softened rice paper, fold over once, tuck in sides then roll up to fully enclose, including a coriander leaf or a few chives in the last roll.

HEAT oil in a heavy frypan and fry wraps over medium heat for about $1^1/_2$-2 minutes on each side until crisp and fish is cooked through. (To test, poke a sharp skewer into centre of parcel – if it meets no resistance and feels springy, fish is cooked.)

Variation: Instead of fish and chilli sauces, try also oyster (see pg 130) or soy sauces.

Over centuries, castaways and explorers from around the globe, traders, whalers, indentured labourers and, later, migrant colonists intermingled with the indigenous Pacific peoples, leaving their mark in looks, traditions and tastes. Racial divisions know no culinary boundaries; while Fijians and Indians are socially separate, Fijians have adopted Indian curries with relish. The Suva markets are a wonderful place to purchase fresh Indian spices,

while excellent French croissants can be savoured in the coffee houses of downtown Port Vila. In the north of this archipelago on the island of Santo, bok choy and other Asian greens can be found in the markets and 'nem' (tiny crisp Vietnamese spring rolls) are sold in general stores of this frontier outpost – a legacy of the thousands of Vietnamese workers who lived here prior to independence.

heaven on earth

fruitful pleasures

Under cover of darkness, there are stories to be told – tales passed down through the generations; an oratory of precious heritage.

The children gather by the fire as the elder begins his journey of words, songs and chants – telling a mythical history that links humans to the gods and the natural world.

Told by his father, his father's father, his father's father's father – and even further back – it is a story that has travelled down the generations, revealing brave deeds, conquests, hierarchies, chiefly titles, place names, proverbs and journeys. The old man's tale takes the listener back to the beginning of time and the first sea voyages across the distant ocean.

So it has been. So it may continue...

cherimoya icecream

• Prepare: 15 minutes • Freeze: 4-5 hours
• Makes about 2 litres (3$\frac{1}{2}$ pints)

This luxurious icecream is a great way to enjoy the tropical cherimoya's short season.

> 2 cups cherimoya flesh
>
> 1 tbsp lemon juice
>
> 2 egg whites
>
> $\frac{1}{2}$ cup sugar
>
> 300ml ($\frac{2}{3}$ pint) cream
>
> 1 tsp vanilla essence

MASH cherimoya flesh with lemon juice. Using an electric beater and a spotlessly clean bowl, beat egg whites and sugar until glossy and stiff.

BEAT cream and vanilla essence to soft peaks in a separate bowl. Fold cream into cherimoya, then fold in egg whites. Freeze until set.

Cook's notes:
• This icecream will keep for 2 weeks. Take out of the freezer and place in the fridge about 15 minutes before you plan to serve it.
• Like avocados, creamy cherimoyas are ready when they show some 'give' when gently squeezed. They are over-ripe if the flesh is browning and there is a slightly 'off' flavour.

lime soufflés

• Prepare: 15 minutes • Cook: 10 minutes
• Makes 6-8 individual soufflés

Home-made Lime Curd✿ makes fast work of these light-as-air soufflés. They can be assembled, ready to cook, 2-3 hours ahead of serving, and they'll stay airborne for at least 15 minutes.

> 2 egg whites, stored at room temperature
>
> $\frac{1}{4}$ cup white sugar
>
> $\frac{1}{2}$ cup Lime Curd✿

WHISK egg whites with sugar to stiff peaks. Carefully reheat lime curd over a gentle heat to avoid 'splitting'.

FOLD hot lime curd into beaten egg whites using a gentle scooping motion.

PLACE 6-8 ramekins or heatproof cups on a baking tray. Divide mixture between ramekins. Chill until ready to cook (up to 3 hours).

HEAT oven to 200°C (400°F/gas 6). Bake soufflés for 10 minutes until risen and lightly golden. Serve at once.

Cook's note: Lime Curd is one of those eminently useful chilled pantry items, great for impromptu desserts:
• Use it to sandwich crisp biscuits such as Sugar Lime Cookies✿.
• Fill a cooked sweet pastry shell with curd and top with fresh fruits.
• Mix with chilled whipped cream as a filling for profiteroles or meringues.

lime soufflé at top, lychee sorbet served with a wedge of fresh cherimoya below

lychee sorbet

- Prepare: 5 minutes • Freeze: 8 hours
- Makes 3 cups

Canned lychees make fast work of this beautiful sorbet. Its wonderful creamy texture belies a lack of fat. Instead, egg white and a little gelatine achieve the same effect.

1 x 565g (20oz) can lychees, including juice

1 tsp gelatine

3 tbsp maple syrup or honey

2 tsp minced fresh ginger

1 tbsp lemon juice

1 very fresh free-range egg white

PLACE lychee juice and gelatine in a small pot or microwave bowl. Heat to dissolve (microwave on HIGH for 1 minute).

PUREE with the lychees and all other ingredients except the egg white. Blend until smooth and creamy in texture.

FREEZE in a shallow container for at least 8 hours. (It can be made to this stage up to 2 weeks in advance.)

UP TO 6 hours before serving, scoop the frozen mixture into the bowl of a food-processor bowl, add egg white and blend until white and fluffy. Refreeze for at least 1 hour to firm.

Variation: Try this sorbet using canned mangos or nectarines in place of lychees. While the flavour will be different (lychees are wonderfully exotic), it's a great technique and allows the flavour of whatever fruit used to shine through.

Cook's note: Sorbet loses its creamy, scooping consistency after prolonged freezing, which is why I choose to blend in the egg white close to the time I plan to serve it.

COCOA
(Cacao theobroma)

Hanging like lanterns,
the golden or orange pods of
the cocoa tree stand out among the
jungle's lush green foliage, and are
adored by children for whom sweet
flavours, with the exception of fruit,
are a rare pleasure.

Each cocoa pod contains about 40
beans, which are coated in a sweet,
creamy, white flesh. Village children
love to suck out this juicy treat
before the beans are laid out
to dry. Dried beans are toasted,
cooled and then ground to a sticky
paste. This is added to boiling
water with lots of sugar and
coconut cream or UHT milk to make
a much-loved drink known in Samoa
as 'koko'. While native to South
America, cocoa trees, like vanilla,
now grow wild throughout many
Pacific Islands and are
cultivated commercially in Samoa.

fruit salad with ginger lemongrass syrup

- **Prepare: 5 minutes** • **Cook: 5 minutes**
- **Serves 4-6**

This zesty syrup makes a great base for fresh or poached fruits.

Ginger Lemongrass Syrup: $3/4$ cup canned lychee juice or water; 1 tsp minced fresh ginger; 1 tbsp lime juice; 6 stalks lemongrass, cut in 3cm (1in) lengths and bruised with a large knife; $1/4$ cup (tightly packed) grated palm sugar (see pg 143) or brown sugar

1 x 565g (20oz) can lychees

1 punnet strawberries, hulled (halved if large)

4 just-ripe kiwifruit, peeled and sliced

PREPARE syrup by combining ingredients in a pot. Cover and bring to a boil. Simmer 5 minutes. Cool.

MIX syrup through fruit. Chill for at least 1 hour (up to 4) before serving.

fresh pineapple with kiwifruit and lychees

- **Prepare: 5 minutes** • **Serves 4**

1 ripe pineapple, peeled, cored and chopped into wedges

4 kiwifruit, peeled and sliced

1 x 565g (20oz) can lychees

1 tsp liquid honey

COMBINE fruit in a serving bowl. Drizzle with honey and leave for at least 30 minutes or up to 4 hours in the fridge before serving.

tangelo and lemongrass jellies

- Prepare: 15 minutes • Cook: 5 minutes
- Serves 6-8

The subtle flavour of lemongrass takes the melt-in-the-mouth pleasure of jelly into a new realm. Six teaspoons of gelatine will set three cups of liquid quite firmly. Here, the addition of rum and lime juice gives the jellies a softer, more 'spoonable' texture.

$^1/_2$ cup palm sugar (see pg 143) or brown sugar

1 cup boiling water

3 tbsp minced lemongrass or finely grated rind 3 limes (no pith)

6 tsp gelatine

2 tbsp rum

$^1/_4$ cup fresh lime juice

2 cups freshly squeezed tangelo or orange juice

To serve (optional): finely chopped fresh fruits, fresh orange juice

MIX sugar with boiling water and lemongrass or lime rind and stir to dissolve. Simmer for 5 minutes.

COMBINE gelatine with rum and lime juice and stir into hot liquid to thoroughly dissolve. Mix in tangelo or orange juice.

POUR into 6-8 small moulds. Cover and chill for 3-4 hours until set.

UNMOULD jellies onto serving plates and garnish with finely chopped fresh fruits and a spoonful of fresh orange juice.

tangelo and lemongrass jelly at top.coconut pavlova below

individual coconut pavlovas

- Prepare: 15 minutes • Cook: 45 minutes
- Makes 6-8 individual pavlovas

Ensure there is not a skerrick of fat on the beater or mixing bowl when making meringue. Cooked meringue, without the topping, will keep fresh in an airtight container for up to a week.

6 egg whites (at least a week old), stored at room temperature

pinch salt

1½ cups caster sugar

2 tsp cornflour

1 tsp white vinegar

1 cup coarse-thread coconut

300ml (½ pint) cream, chilled

1 tbsp icing sugar, plus extra for dusting

1 tsp vanilla essence

½ cup passionfruit pulp or puréed mango in syrup

6 kiwifruit, peeled and finely chopped

HEAT oven (don't use fan setting) to 170°C (325°F/gas 3). Line a baking tray with baking paper.

PLACE egg whites in bowl of an electric mixer. Add salt and sugar and beat for about 10 minutes until mixture is shiny, glossy and very thick. Whisk in cornflour and vinegar, then fold in coconut.

DROP big spoonfuls of the mixture onto the prepared tray, making 6 to 8 individual pavlovas. Swirl meringue with a fork or spatula.

BAKE for 5 minutes then reduce temperature to 130°C (260°F/gas 1) and cook a further 40 minutes, until shell is crisp to the touch. Turn off oven and leave pavlovas to cool in oven.

WHIP cream to soft peaks with the icing sugar and vanilla. Place a spoonful on meringues, spoon over passionfruit pulp and scatter over kiwifruit. Serve, dusted with icing sugar.

PALM SUGAR

A number of different palms yield palm sugar, but all take 15-20 years to produce harvestable sap. The most prized, to my mind, is the toddy palm, which produces the splendid, almost fudgy, jaggery of Burma. Through much of Asia and parts of the Pacific, palm sugar is used as a sweetener. It can be bought in jars as a concentrated syrup, or in solid blocks which are produced by further boiling down the palm sap. Cylindrical cakes of sugar are formed in bamboo sections, while the half-round cakes are made by pouring the hot concentrated syrup into coconut shells. Palm sugar has a rich caramel flavour. If unavailable, the best substitute is made with equal parts brown sugar and maple syrup.

pineapple and banana sorbet

• Prepare: 10 minutes • Freeze: 8 hours
• Makes about 2 litres (3$\frac{1}{2}$ pints)

1 cup sugar

$\frac{1}{2}$ cup water

1 medium pineapple, cored, peeled and chopped

2 bananas, peeled and chopped

1 tbsp lemon juice

1 egg white

HEAT sugar and water, stirring until sugar dissolves. Boil 10 minutes and cool.

PUREE pineapple flesh with bananas and lemon juice to a smooth texture. Blend in cooled syrup.

FREEZE in a shallow container for at least 8 hours. (It can be made to this stage up to 2 weeks in advance.)

UP TO 6 hours before serving, scoop the frozen mixture into a food-processor bowl, add egg white and blend until white and fluffy. Refreeze for at least 1 hour to firm. (See *Cook's note*, pg 139.)

strawberry vanilla sauce

PUREE 1 punnet strawberries, hulled, with 2 tbsp icing sugar and 1 tsp vanilla essence until smooth. Chill until ready to use. Use within 24 hours. Makes 1$\frac{3}{4}$ cups.

kiwifruit sauce

PLACE 2 peeled kiwifruit, 2-3 tbsp (to taste) sugar and 1 tbsp lime or lemon juice in a food processor. Purée in short bursts to prevent seeds pulverising (or sauce will be bitter). Chill. It will keep for 2-3 days. Makes about 1 cup.

macadamia feuilleté with caramelised banana topping

• Prepare: 15 minutes • Cook: 20 minutes
• Serves 6-8

Crisp filo pastry layered with ground macadamia nuts and sugar makes a perfect base for a range of toppings and desserts. Caramelised bananas, as shown here, are delicious, but mangos or apricots could also be used. The cooked feuilleté can also be served layered with whipped cream and fresh fruit.

Filo Feuilleté: 4 tbsp ground macadamia nuts or almond meal, 4 tbsp sugar, 6 filo sheets, 50g (2oz) melted butter

Caramelised Banana Topping: 3 firm bananas, peeled and thinly angle-sliced; 2 tbsp caster sugar

To serve (optional): Preserved Passionfruit Syrup✿ or Kiwifruit Sauce✿

HEAT oven to 180°C (350°F/gas 4). Line a baking tray with baking paper.

COMBINE nuts or almond meal and sugar. Lay a sheet of pastry on prepared tray. Brush with butter and sprinkle with a thin coating of nut-and-sugar mixture. Repeat with remaining filo sheets. Press down to compact layers. Cut out into 6-8 squares or rounds, discarding excess. Place baking paper on top to cover and then weigh down with another oven tray. Bake for 20 minutes until pastry is crisp and pale golden.

HEAT GRILL. Cover filo bases with banana slices, making sure bases are completely covered or else they will burn. Sprinkle with sugar and place under a hot grill to caramelise.

SERVE hot or at room temperature with Preserved Passionfruit Syrup or Kiwifruit Sauce.

Cook's note: Filo bases can be cooked a day or two ahead of time and stored in an airtight container.

passionfruit and vanilla terrine

• Prepare: 15 minutes • Serves 8-10

This wonderful dessert has a silky texture and unctuous, creamy flavour but, thanks to the combination of cream and yoghurt, is not too rich. Serve it sliced, scooped or in individual moulds. Make it a day or two before you plan to serve it and store in the fridge.

> 600ml (1 pint) cream
>
> $^{3}/_{4}$ cup sugar
>
> 2-3 strips lime rind, cut with a peeler (no pith), plus 2 tbsp lime juice
>
> 2 tsp vanilla essence
>
> 6 tsp gelatine
>
> 600ml (1 pint) Greek yoghurt
>
> $^{1}/_{4}$ cup strained Preserved Passionfruit Syrup⊙, plus passionfruit pulp or extra syrup to serve

HEAT cream and sugar with lime rind and vanilla. Bring to a simmer, remove from heat and discard lime rind.

DISSOLVE gelatine in lime juice and stir into the hot cream. Whisk in yoghurt and Preserved Passionfruit Syrup until evenly combined.

TRANSFER mixture to a 2 litre (3½ pint) container (an icecream carton works fine), or chill in individual moulds lined with plastic wrap. Chill for at least 3 hours until firm.

SERVE in scoops, or loosen edges and unmould. Accompany with passionfruit pulp or Preserved Passionfruit Syrup.

Cook's note: Terrine will keep in the fridge for up to 4 days.

coconut icecream

• Prepare: 15 minutes • Freeze: at least 4 hours
• Makes about 2 litres (3½ pints)

This icecream is easy to make without an icecream maker. All kinds of flavourings can be used; you may also like to add half a cup of ground chocolate-coated coffee beans.

> 6 eggs
>
> 1 cup caster sugar
>
> 1 tbsp boiling water
>
> 1½ cups cream, chilled
>
> ½ cup coconut cream
>
> 2 tsp vanilla essence
>
> 1 cup toasted thread coconut

SEPARATE eggs. Mix yolks, three-quarters of the sugar and the boiling water for about 5 minutes until mixture is pale and forms thick ribbons when the beater is lifted.

IN A SEPARATE BOWL, whisk cream and coconut cream to soft peaks with vanilla essence.

IN ANOTHER BOWL – using a clean beater and blades – whisk egg whites with remaining sugar until thick and glossy (about 5 minutes).

USING a large, flat spoon, gently fold together the three mixtures with the coconut. Pour into a container and cover. Freeze until firm – at least 4 hours.

Cook's notes:
• Use within 2 weeks. Take icecream out of the freezer and place in the fridge about 15 minutes before you plan to serve it.
• There are many types of dried coconut, made from the white part of the kernel, used in cooking. Thick, flat pieces of coconut are known as coconut flakes, long thin threads are known as thread coconut, and the fine sawdust-textured common coconut is called desiccated.

vanilla flowers at top,
passionfruit and vanilla terrine below

VANILLA
(vanilla tahitensis/planifolia)

The allure of vanilla rests
deep in the human psyche.
At birth, the same aroma
is released from the aureole around
the mother's nipple, thus attracting
the babe to suckle. Children can
be easily calmed by a drop of
vanilla in their milk, or a vanilla pod
placed under their pillow does
the same trick.

Vanilla — the power to soothe

Vanilla tahitensis is native to the
rainforests of Tahiti. Today, vanilla
vines can be found growing wild
in lush valleys throughout the
Pacific. After harvest, the green
pods undergo a lengthy curing
process, not unlike that required
by tea. This releases their exotic
aroma and flavour. Store vanilla
pods in your sugar jar.

mango cheesecake

• Prepare: 15 minutes • Serves 8-10

This simple cheesecake, combining cream-cheese and canned mangos, makes a rich and impressive dessert. Serve in wedges or use a sharp, round cutter to stamp out rounds from the chilled, set cheesecake. It's delicious served with Mango Passion Sauce✿ or Preserved Passionfruit Syrup✿.

$1^{1}/_{2}$ cups plain sweet biscuit crumbs

$1^{1}/_{2}$ cups finely chopped macadamias or toasted almonds

100g (4oz) butter, melted

3 tsp gelatine

$^{1}/_{4}$ cup water

250g (9oz) cream-cheese

$^{1}/_{2}$ cup caster sugar

$^{3}/_{4}$ cup cream

2 x 425g (15oz) cans mangos in juice, drained

$^{1}/_{4}$ cup finely chopped crystallised ginger

MIX biscuit crumbs and nuts together. Stir in butter and combine evenly. Press into a 23-25cm (9-10in) ring tin. Chill.

HEAT gelatine and water in a small pot and stir well to dissolve. Place in a food-processor bowl with cream-cheese, caster sugar, cream and half the mangos. Purée until smooth. Finely chop remaining mangos and stir into cream-cheese mixture with ginger. Pour into prepared base. Chill for 4-5 hours.

Cook's note: Store cheesecake in a sealed container. It will keep for 2-3 days in the fridge.

mango cheesecake at top,
fresh pineapple below

frozen coconut and pineapple cake

- Prepare: 15 minutes • Freeze: 5-6 hours
- Serves 6-8

Here's one of those terrific recipes that looks and tastes really impressive but is a cinch to prepare. Serve with Kiwifruit Sauce✿, Strawberry Vanilla Sauce✿ or Preserved Passionfruit Syrup✿.

3 egg whites (stored at room temperature)

pinch salt

$^1\!/_2$ cup sugar

300ml ($^1\!/_2$ pint) cream

1 tsp vanilla essence

1 cup lightly toasted thread coconut

$^3\!/_4$ cup finely chopped glacé pineapple

1 tbsp lemon juice

$^1\!/_2$ cup chopped, toasted macadamia nuts or toasted almonds (optional)

$^1\!/_4$ cup Cocoribe, Malibu or white rum

WHIP egg whites with salt until they form soft peaks (you will need an electric beater and a spotlessly clean bowl to do this). Slowly add the sugar and beat until very stiff.

WHIP cream and vanilla in a separate bowl until cream forms peaks. Fold in coconut, pineapple, lemon juice, nuts and rum. Fold in the beaten egg whites.

LINE a loaf tin, or a 20cm (8in) cake tin with a removable base, with plastic wrap. Spoon mixture into tin.

COVER and freeze for 5-6 hours or until firm. Unmould onto a plate; serve in slices.

Cook's note: This delicious cake can be frozen for up to a month.

mature coconut at top, frozen coconut and pineapple cake below

grilled pineapple with rum and star anise

- Prepare: 10 minutes, plus marinating
- Cook: 5 minutes • Serves 4

This simple treatment for fresh pineapple makes a light, refreshing dessert. Choose a heavy, firm pineapple with a pleasant, fruity aroma.

> 1 pineapple, peeled and cut in half lengthwise
>
> $1/2$ cup passionfruit pulp or Preserved Passionfruit Syrup✿
>
> $1/2$ cup rum
>
> 4 whole star anise, plus extra for garnish
>
> $1/4$ cup sugar

REMOVE core from pineapple halves and cut each half into 6-7 slices. Drizzle passionfruit pulp in the bottom of a shallow baking dish. Place pineapple on top and pour over rum. Scatter over star anise. Marinate for up to 4 hours or overnight in the fridge.

HEAT grill. Sprinkle pineapple with sugar and grill for about 5 minutes until lightly browned. Serve pineapple with the cooking syrup and a garnish of star anise.

Cook's notes:
- All sorts of fruits take well to this marinating and grilling treatment. Try stone fruits, mangos, feijoas, bananas and papaya. Either halve fruit or cut into wedges, removing skin and any inedible seeds or stones.
- Whole star anise is a star-shaped spice with a licorice flavour popular in Vietnamese and Chinese cooking.

fried bananas with lychees and passionfruit

- Prepare: 5 minutes • Cook: 6-8 minutes
- Serves 4-6

This is one of those great impromptu dishes that transforms a can of lychees and some fresh bananas into a quick, luscious dessert. The small finger bananas are the best to use for this dish, as they hold their shape well when cooked.

> 6 small finger bananas
>
> 3 tbsp butter
>
> 3 tbsp brown sugar
>
> 1 x 565g (20oz) can lychees, including $1/2$ cup juice
>
> juice $1/2$ lime
>
> 2 tbsp passionfruit pulp or Preserved Passionfruit Syrup✿

PEEL bananas and cut in half lengthwise. Heat butter and sugar in a heavy frypan and fry banana for about a minute on each side until lightly golden. Divide between plates.

ADD lychees to pan, along with lime juice, the lychee juice and the passionfruit pulp or Preserved Passionfruit Syrup. Simmer for a minute or two until syrupy. Remove from heat. Spoon lychees and pan liquids over the bananas.

To the outsider, life in the remote outer islands of the Pacific appears as a paradise of gin-clear coral waters teeming with seafood, and white-sand beaches fringed with coconut palms. The reality, on the contrary, is a tenuous existence ruled by wind and sea; where resourcefulness and ingenuity are the key to survival. Even today, the trappings of the West amount to little in these distant outposts – maybe a few sheets of rusting

corrugated iron or an old tarpaulin, rolls of fishing nylon and metal hooks, the odd kerosene lamp, soap, matches and light clothing. Far out in the remote islands, where contact with the Western world may be limited to a yearly visit from a supply vessel or the occasional passing yacht, the daily rituals and rhythms of traditional Pacific life continue much as they have done for centuries.

useful side dishes

caramelised pineapple and kumara
Peel 8 yellow kumara. Cut into thin slices and cook in boiling, salted water for 5 minutes. Drain well. Place in a shallow roasting dish with 1 peeled, fresh pineapple, flesh cut into 1cm ($\frac{1}{2}$in) thick rounds, then each slice cut into 6 wedges. Spread out to a single layer (you may need two dishes). Mix through 3 tbsp oil (or spray with a little oil) and sprinkle with 3 tbsp brown sugar. Season with salt. Bake at 200°C (400°F/gas 6) for about 40 minutes until starting to brown. Serves 8.

chinese slaw
Place $\frac{1}{4}$ very finely shredded red cabbage in a bowl with a pinch each of sugar and salt. Work sugar and salt through the cabbage with your hands to release the juices. Toss through 1 peeled and finely shredded carrot; 1 stalk celery, cut thinly on an angle; $\frac{1}{4}$ cup currants soaked in $\frac{1}{4}$ cup orange juice to plump; 2 spring onions, thinly sliced; 2 tbsp sesame seeds, toasted; juice 1 lime or lemon and 1 tbsp fish sauce. Serves 4-6.

coconut rice
Place 1 cup long-grain rice in a pot with $\frac{1}{4}$ cup toasted desiccated coconut, 2 cups cold water, $\frac{1}{2}$ tsp salt, finely grated rind $\frac{1}{2}$ lime (no pith) or 2 kaffir lime leaves. Stir and bring to a boil. Cover and reduce heat to lowest setting. Cook for 12 minutes. Remove from heat without lifting lid and stand a further 12 minutes. Fluff with a fork. Serves 6.

cucumber and banana raita
Finely dice $\frac{1}{2}$ telegraph cucumber and combine with 2 tbsp chopped mint and 1 clove peeled and crushed garlic. When ready to serve, add $\frac{1}{4}$ cup plain yoghurt, 1 large peeled and diced banana and 2-3 tbsp orange juice. Season with salt and freshly ground black pepper. (Cucumber will get watery if held with dressing on.) Serves 4.

fresh banana salad
Peel and angle-cut 4 firm bananas in thin slices. Toss through $\frac{1}{2}$ cup lime or lemon juice, $1\frac{1}{2}$ cups toasted thread coconut (see pg 146) and $\frac{1}{4}$ cup fresh chopped coriander. Serves 6-8.

fried plantain, cashews and coconut
Boil 2 green plantain for 15 minutes. Cool, peel and angle-slice into pieces about 1.5cm ($\frac{1}{2}$in) thick. Shallow-fry in oil for 2-3 minutes each side until golden. Drain and toss with $\frac{1}{2}$ cup chopped cashew nuts and $\frac{1}{2}$ cup toasted thread coconut (see pg 146). At serving time, sprinkle with salt and squeeze over juice of a lime or lemon. (If plantain are unavailable, substitute with peeled kumara.) Serves 4-6.

fried spiced tomatoes
Cut 3 large tomatoes into thick slices. Combine 1 tsp curry powder, 1 tsp brown sugar, $\frac{1}{2}$ tsp salt and a generous grind of black pepper in a small bowl. Dip sliced tomatoes into spice mix to lightly coat. Fry in a little butter on each side until starting to soften. Serves 4-6.

green papaya and vermicelli salad
The papaya must have a very green skin or it will become mushy when grated. If green papaya is unavailable, use fresh pineapple instead. Cover 200g (7oz) bean thread vermicelli (see pg 123) with boiling water and stand for 5 minutes. Rinse under cold water and drain. Snip into smaller lengths with scissors. Coarsely grate $\frac{1}{2}$ peeled and deseeded green papaya, or $\frac{1}{4}$ fresh pineapple, peeled and chopped into thin matchsticks. Place in a large mixing bowl with the noodles; $\frac{1}{2}$ cup chopped coriander; 2 spring onions, cut in long, thin strips and 1 cup coarsely chopped roasted peanuts. To make the dressing, combine 3 tbsp fish sauce; 5 tbsp lime or lemon juice; 1 tsp sugar and 2 small red chillies, deseeded, pith removed and very finely chopped. Toss through salad. Serves 6-8.

jungle herb salad
Combine a handful each of fresh basil leaves and Vietnamese mint (or regular mint leaves) with 2 handfuls beet leaves, watercress or baby spinach, $\frac{1}{2}$ packet bean sprouts and 2 small red chillies, deseeded, pith removed and finely chopped. When ready to serve, toss with juice of 1 lime, 1 tbsp fish sauce and a pinch of sugar. Serves 4.

lightly cooked asian greens
Cut 4-6 whole baby bok choy into quarters, lengthwise, and wash well. Heat 1 tbsp sesame oil in a wok or pot. Add wet vegetables and a grating of fresh ginger, cover and cook over high heat for 2-3 minutes until wilted, stirring occasionally. Season to taste. Serves 4.

red onion, pineapple and watercress salad
Toss together $\frac{1}{4}$ red onion, peeled and finely sliced; $\frac{1}{4}$ fresh pineapple, peeled and finely sliced; 1 bunch watercress, coarse stems removed; juice 1 lime; 1 tsp sugar; 1 tbsp fish sauce and serve at once. Serves 4-6.

sesame grilled vegetables
Briefly boiling vegetables makes for shorter grill time and less risk of burning before they are cooked through. They also absorb flavourings more readily. Drop 3 zucchinis, angle-cut in 2cm (1in) slices, into a pot of boiling, salted water with 3 peppers (red/yellow/green) deseeded, pith removed and cut in large dice and 2 handfuls green beans, halved, ends removed. Cook for 2 minutes. Drain and cool under cold water. Drain well and mix through 1 tbsp sesame oil and 2 tsp minced fresh ginger. Chill if not using at once. Heat a barbecue hot-plate or grill. Barbecue or

grill for 3-4 minutes until lightly browned. Transfer to a serving plate and sprinkle with 2 tbsp toasted sesame seeds. Serves 4-6.

sweet-potato mash

Peel and quarter 4 medium potatoes and 2 large kumaras and boil in salted water until tender. Mash until fine, adding a knob of butter and a splash of olive oil. Season to taste with salt and white pepper. Serves 4-6.

wilted watercress

Wash stems of a large bunch fresh watercress. Heat a heavy pan with 2 tbsp olive oil. Add wet watercress and cook for 2-3 minutes until leaves are wilted and stems are tender. Season with a dash of salt. Serves 4.

pacific flavours

asian barbecue sauce

Mix 1/4 cup oyster sauce (see pg 130), 3 tbsp sake (see pg 81) or mirin, 2 tbsp sweet chilli sauce, 1 tbsp fresh minced ginger and 1 tbsp minced coriander. Sauce will keep in a sealed container in the fridge for a couple of days. Makes 1/2 cup.

avocado chilli salsa

Combine diced flesh 1 just-ripe avocado with 1 tbsp chopped coriander, 1 tbsp Thai sweet chilli sauce, 1 tbsp lemon juice and salt and freshly ground black pepper. Cover securely and chill until ready to serve. Makes about 1 cup.

candied hibiscus flowers

Beat egg white until fluffy. Remove petals from fresh, unsprayed hibiscus flowers and drop into egg white. Brush each with your finger to lightly coat. Wipe off excess moisture with your finger – surface should just be lightly dampened. Shake in caster sugar to coat. Spread coated flowers on a baking tray and bake in a very slow oven about 140°C (275°F/gas 1) for about 1 hour until crisp and dry. Store in an airtight container; they will keep for weeks.

cashew and mustard salsa

Purée together 2 tbsp tarragon vinegar; 1/2 tsp chilli powder; 1 cup water; 2 cups roasted, salted cashews; 1 tsp French mustard; 1 tsp honey; 3 tbsp lemon juice; 1/2 cup oil and 1 tsp fine black pepper until smooth and creamy. Salsa will keep for up to 1 week in the fridge. Makes about 2 1/2 cups.

chilli coriander pesto

Use to add flavour to noodle and rice dishes, mix into mayonnaise or oil-based salad dressings and as a flavouring or spread for sandwiches, pies and fillings. Wash a big bunch of fresh coriander, including the roots. Place in a heat-proof bowl and pour over boiling water to cover. Drain at once. Place in a blender with 2 cloves peeled garlic; 2 small chillies, deseeded and pith removed; 1/2 tsp salt; 1/2 tsp finely grated lemon rind (no pith); 1/4 cup roasted peanuts and 1/2 cup salad oil. Purée together until mixture forms a smooth paste. Place in a jar and cover surface with a layer of olive oil to prevent pesto from drying out. Keeps for 10-12 days in the fridge. Makes 1 cup.

chilli jam

Place 4 peeled and chopped onions in a heavy pot with 8 peeled and crushed cloves garlic; 8 small red chillies, stems removed; 2 red peppers, deseeded, pith removed and cut in strips, and 1 cup vegetable oil. Cook slowly for 30-40 minutes until onion is very soft. Purée. Return to pot with 2 tbsp tamarind concentrate, 1/4 cup brown sugar and 2 tbsp fish sauce and cook a further 45-50 minutes until very thick, stirring occasionally to make sure mixture does not catch. Place in a jar and cover surface with a layer of olive oil to prevent contents from drying out. Jam will keep for over a month in the fridge. Makes 1 large jarful.

chilli lime dipping sauce

Combine 1/4 cup Thai sweet chilli sauce, 1 tbsp fish sauce, juice 1/2 lemon and a little chopped coriander. Makes 1/3 cup.

chilli sauce

Purée 10 cloves garlic, peeled, with 3 tbsp fresh minced ginger; 4 double kaffir lime leaves, central stems removed and leaves finely shredded; 1 tbsp minced lemongrass and 1 cup fresh coriander. Place in a pot with 2 tbsp fish sauce, 2 tbsp tamari (see pg 102) or light soy sauce, 1 tbsp rice wine or cider vinegar and 1 cup Thai sweet chilli sauce. Simmer for 5-8 minutes. Leave to cool. Sauce will keep in the fridge for several months. Makes 1 3/4 cups.

eggplant kasundi

Purée 1 large hand (225g/8oz) fresh, peeled ginger with 2 whole heads of garlic, peeled; 12 green chillies, sliced in half lengthwise, deseeded and pith removed, and 1/2 cup malt vinegar to make a paste. Heat 1 cup canola or safflower oil in a very big pot or preserving pan. Add 2 tbsp turmeric; 5 tbsp ground cumin; 2 tbsp chilli powder; 5 tbsp mustard seeds, ground to a powder; 1 tsp fennel seeds, roughly crushed, and 2 peeled and very finely chopped onions. Fry until mixture exudes a fragrant aroma. Add the puréed ginger paste, 2kg (4 1/2lb) washed and diced eggplant, 2 cups malt vinegar, 1 1/4 cups sugar and about 1 1/2 tbsp salt. Cook, covered, over a low heat, stirring occasionally, until the oil floats on the top (about 55 minutes). Bottle in sterilised jars while hot, pouring a thin film of hot oil on the top of each jar to prevent contents from drying out. Cover with screw-top seal lids. Leave for a couple of weeks to allow flavours to develop. Stored in a cool place, it will keep indefinitely. Makes 5 jars.

lime curd

Place 1 cup sugar and finely grated rind 3 limes (no pith) in a pot with $\frac{1}{2}$ cup lime juice and 200g (7oz) unsalted butter, cut into about 10 pieces. Bring to a boil. Remove sugar and butter mixture from heat and whisk in 4 lightly beaten eggs. Place pot over larger pot of boiling water and stir constantly until sauce is thickened. Cool and spoon into containers. Curd will keep for 10 days in the fridge. (Lemons can be used in place of limes or, to make a passionfruit curd, use $\frac{1}{2}$ cup passionfruit pulp.) Makes 2 cups.

lime mayonnaise

Place 1 tsp salt, $\frac{1}{2}$ tsp white pepper, finely grated rind 1 lime (no pith) and $\frac{1}{4}$ cup juice and 3 egg yolks in a food-processor bowl and blend to combine. With motor running, add 1 cup grapeseed oil in a thin stream until a lightly thickened sauce texture is achieved. (If you add too much oil and it gets too thick, you can thin with a little hot water.) Remove central stem from 4 double kaffir lime leaves. Shred leaves finely and pour over boiling water. Strain at once. Blend leaves into mayonnaise. Mayo will keep for 5-6 days in the fridge. Makes $1\frac{1}{4}$ cups.

mint and ginger pesto

Use to add flavour to noodle and rice dishes, mix into mayonnaise or oil-based salad dressings, and as a flavouring or spread for sandwiches, pies and fillings. Into a food processor, place a large handful of mint, stalks removed; 2-3 cloves garlic, peeled; 2 tbsp minced fresh ginger; $\frac{1}{2}$ cup flavourless oil (eg, grapeseed) and a pinch each of salt and freshly ground black pepper. Purée until smooth, adjusting the quantity of oil until it becomes a smooth, soft paste. Keeps

in fridge for about 2 weeks. Spicy greens, such as rocket or watercress, can be used in place of parsley. Makes about 1 cup.

preserved passionfruit syrup

This is a great way to preserve passionfruit – equal volumes of passionfruit and sugar create a rich macerating syrup. Place 1 cup passionfruit pulp in a sterilised jar and pour over 1 cup white or brown sugar. Cover and store in fridge. Shake occasionally over the first day or two until all the sugar dissolves. Keeps in fridge for months. Syrup can be sieved to remove pips if preferred. Makes $1\frac{1}{2}$ cups.

spicy peanut sauce

Purée together 4 cloves garlic, peeled and chopped; 2 tbsp fresh minced ginger; 2 tbsp soy sauce; 2 red chillies, deseeded, pith removed and minced; 2 tbsp fish sauce; $\frac{1}{2}$ cup peanut butter; 2 finely sliced spring onions; handful coriander leaves and 1 cup water. Place in a pot and boil for 5 minutes. Sauce will keep in fridge for about a week. Makes $1\frac{1}{2}$ cups.

tamarind dipping sauce

This is a really useful sauce that will keep for months in the fridge. Use it to spread over fish or chicken before grilling, or mix into dressings or salads. It's yummy mixed through diced, cooked duck or chicken served in a crisp wonton basket. Chop tamarind into 3-4cm ($1\frac{1}{2}$in) pieces. Pour over 2 cups of boiling water, stand for 15 minutes then break up with your hands and rub through a sieve into a pot to remove seeds and skin. Pour another cup boiling water through sieve, pressing well to extract all the pulp you can. Add 2 cups brown sugar, 2 tsp mustard seeds, 1 tsp whole cumin seeds, pinch salt and 2 tbsp minced fresh ginger to tamarind pulp. Bring to a simmer and cook gently for about 30 minutes – stirring frequently to ensure

mix does not catch on the bottom of the pot – until thick and pasty. Store in a sealed jar in the fridge. Makes 2 cups.

teriyaki sauce

Use as a marinade for pork, chicken or fish, or as a sauce to flavour stir-fries and rice and noodle dishes. Place $\frac{1}{2}$ cup soy sauce, $\frac{1}{2}$ cup sake, 2 tbsp minced fresh ginger and $\frac{1}{4}$ cup sugar in a pot. Bring to a boil and simmer gently for 10 minutes. Leave to cool. The sauce will keep for several months in the fridge. Makes 1 cup.

tropical fruit chutney

Remove skin and seeds from 3kg ($6\frac{1}{2}$lb) papaya or mangos and roughly chop the flesh. Place in a large, heavy-bottomed pot. Add $2\frac{1}{2}$ cups brown sugar; 2 onions, peeled and very finely chopped; 3 tbsp crushed garlic; 3 tbsp fresh minced ginger; 1 tbsp cinnamon; 1 tsp fennel seeds, roughly crushed; 6 cardamom pods, roughly crushed; 2 small red chillies, deseeded, pith removed and minced; 2 tbsp mustard seeds (black or yellow); 4 tsp salt and 4 cups white vinegar. Stir to combine and bring to a simmer. Leave to cook gently for about $1\frac{1}{2}$ hours, uncovered, or until the mixture is thick and pulpy. (Stir occasionally to prevent mixture from catching on the bottom of the pot.) Remove cardamom pods. Bottle while still hot into sterilised jars and seal with pop-top lids or wax. Makes 6 jars.

Wasabi lime mayonnaise

Place 1 tsp wasabi powder, 1 tsp salt, $\frac{1}{2}$ tsp white pepper, finely grated rind 1 lime (no pith), plus $\frac{1}{3}$ cup fresh lime or lemon juice and 3 egg yolks in a food-processor bowl and blend to combine. With motor running, add 1 cup grapeseed oil in a thin stream until a lightly thickened sauce texture is achieved. (If you add too much oil and it gets too thick, you can thin with a little hot water.) Store in a jar; it keeps for 5-6 days in the fridge. Makes $1\frac{1}{2}$ cups.

glossary

banana flower

The male part of the banana plant is a cone of red leaves, enclosing the long stems from which the bananas grow. These leaves can be sliced for salads or stir-fries or used (like the green leaves) for wrapping food to be cooked.

dried rice noodles

Known also as rice sticks or rice vermicelli, these noodles are soaked before using. Thin varieties can be soaked in warm water until softened, then added to stir-fries, salads and soups; thick noodles should be softened in boiling water. They can also be deep-fried in hot oil until they puff up.

enoki mushrooms

These little clusters of pale, skinny mushrooms are native to Japan. They are favoured as a mild-tasting garnish for soups and stir-fries.

fresh rice noodles

Sold unchilled, often by the checkout at Asian supermarkets, these fresh noodles have a silky, slippery quality. They taste best the day they are made, as with age (and chilling) they lose their elasticity and quickly fall apart when cooked. To use, cover with boiling water, pull apart to separate, then drain at once. Wonderful in stir-fries, soups or stirred through a hot sauce.

fresh udon noodles

These satisfying wheat noodles are sold fresh from the chiller in Asian food stores. Cook for 1-2 minutes in salted, boiling water. Drain, rinse in cold water then drain thoroughly again.

japanese radish

Otherwise known as daikon, this long, white winter radish has a mildly peppery taste and crisp texture. Use within 1-2 days of purchase; grate or shred for salads or raw fish dishes.

kumara leaves

Unlike potato leaves, which are poisonous, the leaves of *ipomoea batatas* – sold in bunches in Asian markets – are a delicious and nutritious green. Discard any tough stems and cook like spinach.

miso

This fermented bean paste, made with soy beans, rice barley or rye, is important in Japanese cooking for making miso soup, as a salad dressing and as a flavouring in simmered dishes. In general, the lighter the colour, the milder the flavour. Miso is a rich source of protein, B vitamins and minerals. It will keep for years in a cool, dry place.

nori

Nori is a type of seaweed, known as laver. Nori sheets may be dark brown or deep green, and are usually sold as 'sushi grade', which means they have been toasted. (Untoasted nori is tough, tasteless and limp.) Sushi nori sheets are sold in packets at most supermarkets and all Asian food stores. Shredded nori is useful for salads or garnishes. Unopened, nori will keep indefinitely.

rice flour

Rice flour is made by grinding dry rice and used in puddings, cakes and biscuits. When used as a coating and fried, it gives a crisp crust.

rice paper

Made of rice-and-water paste, rice paper is sold in packets which contain lots of sheets. It is brittle and fragile when dry. Check the packet when you buy to ensure sheets are undamaged, and handle carefully. The basket-weave pattern on the sheets comes from the bamboo mats the rice paste is dried on. Once moistened, the sheets become flexible wrappers which can be eaten raw, fried or baked. To soften, dip sheets into very hot water, count to 2, remove and place on a clean, damp cloth. It will soften in about a minute. If the wrapper starts to disintegrate when you roll it, it is too wet – you may need to practise a few times to get the hang of it.

vietnamese mint

Once established, this prolific plant grows like a weed. It has a spicy flavour with citrussy overtones and can be used as a substitute for mint or coriander.

wasabi

Native to Japan and cultivated in New Zealand, the root of this plant is used as a traditional condiment for sushi and sashimi. Wasabi is usually purchased as a paste, or as a dry powder, which is mixed like mustard. Its powerful heat provides a sinus-clearing hit.

white rice vinegar

Made from fermented rice, white rice vinegar has a mild, sweet taste and is good in Asian dishes or as a replacement for lemon juice in dressings. If unavailable, diluted white wine or cider vinegar can be substituted.

whole cloves

The aromatic, dried unopened buds of *syzyium aromaticum*, a member of the myrtle family, has been used in China since the 3rd-century BC. The addition of 1-2 whole cloves to dishes – sweet and savoury – adds a fragrant spiciness.

umu

Throughout Melanesia and Polynesia earth ovens – known by different cultures as umu, lovo, mumu, umu ahinaa and hangi, play a central part in cooking and feasting. Aside from the hangi, which is cooked in a deep earth pit, all other earth ovens are made in a shallow pit with hot rocks as the heat source. The food is wrapped in leaves and placed onto the hot rocks with more rocks and a layer of leaves and sometimes soil on top. It cooks for several hours, emerging with a rich smoky flavour.

index

NAURU
• Yaren

KIRIBATI

ADMIRALTY
Is.

PAPUA
NEW GUINEA

• Bougainville

SOLOMON
ISLANDS

TUVALU
Is.

Port
moresby

• Honiara

SANTA CRUZ
Is.

ROTUMA

WESTERN
SAMOA

SAN
CRISTOBAL

BANKS Is.

• Apia

CORAL
SEA

• Uila

TONGA

Suva

FIJI
Is.

Nuku'alofa

NEW CALEDONIA

LOYALTY
Is.

Noumea

AUSTRALIA

• Brisbane

NORFOLK Is.

Sydney

Canberra

NEW
ZEALAND

Auckland

TASMAN
SEA

Wellington

Hobart

Christchurch

TASMANIA

CHATHAM
Is.